A



# All American Stories

C. G. DRAPER

**All American Stories A**



Pearson Education, 10 Bank Street, White Plains, NY 10606

Vice president, primary and secondary editorial: Ed Lamprich
Senior development editor: Lauren Weidenman
Vice president, director of design and production: Rhea Banker
Executive managing editor: Linda Moser
Production editor: Lynn Contrucci
Senior art director: Elizabeth Carlson
Vice president, marketing: Kate McLoughlin
Senior manufacturing buyer: Edith Pullman
Cover design: Lissi Sigillo
Cover art: Thomas Moran (1837–1926), The Grand Canyon of the Yellowstone, 1872. Oil on canvas, 84 × 144¼ in. (231.0 × 266.3 cm). Lent by the Department of the Interior Museum. Smithsonian American Art Museum, Washington, DC. Photo from Smithsonian American Art Museum, Washington, DC/Art Resource, New York
Text design: Elizabeth Carlson
Text composition: Rainbow Graphics
Text fonts: Franklin Gothic Book and Minion
Illustrations: John Edens: "A Cub-Pilot's Education"; Tom LaPadula: "Love of Life"; Rob Lawson: "The Gift of the Magi" and "Of the Coming of John"; Isidre Mones: "How I Went to the Mines"; Jesus Redondo: "The Tell-Tale Heart"; Howard Simpson: "The Lady, or the Tiger?"

**Library of Congress Cataloging-in-Publication Data**

All American stories / [edited] by C.G. Draper.
p. cm.
Includes index.
ISBN 0-13-192986-0
1. English language—Textbooks for foreign speakers. 2. Short stories, American—Adaptations. 3. Readers (Secondary) I. Draper, C. G.
PE1128.A365 2006
428.6′4—dc22

2004026234



Printed in the United States of America
4 5 6 7 8 9 10—VG—09 08 07

# Contents

# To the Student

The stories in this book were written many years ago by seven of America's most famous writers. Some words and sentences in the stories have been changed. These changes make the stories easier to understand for students learning English as a second language.

The introductory unit—"What Is a Short Story?"—is different from Units 1 to 6. It will help you understand how to read a short story. It explains the words **characters, plot, setting,** and **theme**. It also points out details about these features as it takes you through a story called "The Gift of the Magi," by O. Henry.

In Units 1 to 6, you will find:

- A paragraph about the life of the person who wrote the story.
- A section called "Before You Read." This section introduces you to the story. It gives you important background information. And it tells you the meaning of some words that are important in the story.
- The story itself and pictures that help you understand the story.
- A section called "After You Read." This section contains reading comprehension questions, discussion questions, and an extension activity. It also includes exercises in vocabulary and word study, and gives you practice in writing. In addition, this section gives you activities to help you understand the elements of literature.

Reading this book will help you improve many English language skills: reading, speaking, listening, and writing. You will also learn many things about American history and about the daily life of the country's people many years ago.

Good luck, and good reading!

# What Is a Short Story?

A short story can be short or long. But short stories have these things in common: **characters, plot, setting,** and **theme.** These are called the elements of a short story.

**Characters** are the people or the animals in the story. When you read a good story, you care about the characters. You wonder what will happen to them.

What happens to the characters is the story's **plot.** Things that happen are called events. The plot can have one event or many.

The **setting** is where and when the story happens. Some stories happen in a certain place at a certain time. For example, the setting for a story about the American Civil War would probably be America in the 1860s.

The **theme** is an idea about life that the writer communicates through the story. Not all stories have a theme.

The model story for this book is "The Gift of the Magi" by a writer named O. Henry. This is how you might describe the characters, plot, setting, and theme of the story:

**Characters**
Della and Jim, a young married couple

**Plot**
Two people without money solve the problem of buying gifts for each other.

**Setting**
*Time:* Christmas Eve, long ago
*Place:* an apartment in a city

**Theme**
People who love each other want to make unselfish choices to please each other.

## Character

The most important character in a story is the main character. Stories can have more than one main character. Authors, or writers, have several ways of letting readers get to know story characters. They can describe what a character looks like. They can tell you what the character thinks and feels. They can tell you what the character does and says. You believe in characters when an author shows them to you in realistic ways.

In some stories, the main character develops, or changes, because of what happens in the story. The change the character goes through is usually important to the meaning of the story.

The model story, "The Gift of the Magi," has two main characters: Della and Jim. They are a young married couple. They do not change as a result of what happens in the story. But they learn something important about each other.

## Plot

The plot is the action of the story. It is a series of events that lead from one to the other. The plot usually includes a problem that a character must solve. The problem is usually solved near the end of the story.

The character's problem is at the center of the plot. You read to find out how the character will solve the problem. The author keeps you interested by creating **suspense.** Suspense is a feeling of excitement and curiosity about what will happen next.

Another way authors keep you interested is by surprising you. Sometimes the plot of a story takes a sudden turn at the end. This is called a **surprise ending.**

O. Henry, the author of the model story, was known for his surprise endings. See if you can predict, or guess, the surprise ending as you read the story.

## Setting

The setting is the place and the time of the story. Place can mean a country or a room. Time can mean the year or the hour.

Sometimes an author tells you the setting. Often, you have to figure it out. You can do this by looking for details the author gives you.

In some stories the setting is important. For example, a story about storms in the Caribbean must have the Caribbean as its setting.

Sometimes the setting helps to create **mood,** or a feeling. For example, describing bright sunshine and singing birds can create a happy mood. Describing a cold, rainy night can create a sad mood.

The setting of "The Gift of the Magi" is an apartment in a city. The time of the story is long ago.

## Theme

The theme is the central idea or message that the author communicates through the story. This idea or message usually makes you think about life in general.

Sometimes an author tells you exactly what the theme of a story is. But usually authors let you decide the theme after you have read the story. You might need to think about a story for a while before you can put the theme into words.

Why should you look for the theme of a story? If you try to put a story's theme into words, you will understand the story better. And understanding a story lets you enjoy it more fully.

The theme of the model story, "The Gift of the Magi," can be stated in this sentence: People who love each other want to make unselfish choices to please each other.

# The Gift of the Magi

***Adapted from the story by O. Henry***

**Setting:** The author gives details that tell you about the setting. The furniture in the apartment is "old" and "poor." The door has no doorbell. These details suggest that Della and Jim are poor. Their apartment is probably small.

**Plot:** Della has an idea about how to solve her problem. She gets the idea while combing her hair. What do you predict, or guess, she will do?

**Plot:** Della solves her problem by selling her only treasure—her hair.

Della counted her money three times. She had only one dollar and eighty-seven cents. That was all. And tomorrow would be Christmas. What Christmas gift could she buy with only one dollar and eighty-seven cents? Della lay down on the old couch and cried and cried.

Let's leave Della alone for a while and look at her home. The chairs and tables in the apartment were old and poor. Outside there was a mailbox without mail, and a door without a doorbell. The name on the door said MR. JAMES DILLINGHAM YOUNG—Della's dear husband, Jim.

Della knew that Jim would be home soon. She dried her eyes and stood up. She looked in the mirror. She began to comb her hair for Jim. She felt very sad. She wanted to buy Jim a Christmas gift—something good. But what could she do with one dollar and eighty-seven cents? She combed her hair in front of the mirror and thought. Suddenly she had an idea.

Now, Jim and Della had only two treasures. One was Jim's gold watch. The other was Della's hair. It was long and brown, and fell down her back. Della looked in the mirror a little longer. Her eyes were sad, but then she smiled. She put on her old brown coat and her hat. She ran out of the apartment house and down the street. She stopped in front of a door which said, MME. SOPHRONIE. HAIR OF ALL KINDS. Madame Sophronie was fat and seemed too white. The store was dark.

"Will you buy my hair?" Della asked.

"I buy hair," said Madame. "Take off your hat. Let's see your hair."

Della took off her hat. Her hair fell down like water. Mme. Sophronie lifted Della's hair with a heavy hand. "Twenty dollars," she said.

"Give me the money now!" said Della.

Ah! the next two hours flew past like summer wind. Della shopped in many stores for the right gift for Jim. Then she found it—a chain for his gold watch. It was a good chain, strong and expensive. Della knew the chain would make Jim happy. Jim had a cheap chain for his watch, but this chain was much better. It would look good with the gold watch. The chain cost twenty-one dollars. Della paid for the chain and ran home with eighty-seven cents.

**Setting:** Della looks in many stores for a gift. This suggests that the story takes place in a city, where there are many stores next door to one another. The good watch chain costs twenty-one dollars. This tells you that the story takes place long ago. In Della's day, twenty-one dollars was a lot of money —much more than it is today.

At seven o'clock Della made coffee and started to cook dinner. Jim would be home soon. He was never late. Della heard Jim outside. She looked in the mirror again. "Oh! I hope Jim doesn't kill me!" Della smiled, but her eyes were wet. "But what could I do with only one dollar and eighty-seven cents?"

The door opened, and Jim came in and shut it. His face was thin and quiet. His coat was old, and he had no hat. He was only twenty-two. Jim stood still and looked at Della. He didn't speak. His eyes were strange. Della suddenly felt afraid. She did not understand him. She began to talk very fast. "Oh, Jim, dear, why do you look so strange? Don't look at me like that. I cut my hair and sold it. I wanted to buy you a Christmas gift. It will grow again—don't be angry. My hair grows very fast. Say 'Merry Christmas,' dear, and let's be happy. You don't know what I've got for you—it's beautiful."

**Plot:** Jim looks strange, and Della thinks it's because she has cut her hair. It is, but not because Jim doesn't like the way Della looks. You have to keep reading to find out why Jim is so shocked to see Della's short hair.

"You cut your hair?" Jim spoke slowly.

"I cut it and sold it," Della answered. "Don't you like me now? I'm still me, aren't I?"

"You say that your hair is gone?" Jim asked again.

"Don't look for it, it's gone," Della said. "Be good to me, because it's Christmas. Shall we have dinner now, Jim?"

**Character:** Jim cannot believe that Della has cut her hair. He sees that her hair is gone, yet he asks her twice if she cut it. This helps you understand how shocked Jim is.

Jim seemed to wake up. He smiled. He took Della in his arms.

Let's leave them together for a while. They are happy, rich or poor. Do you know about the Magi? The Magi were wise men who

**Theme:** The author mentions the Magi here and in the story's title. This gives you an idea about the theme. The theme is about giving gifts to show love.

**Plot:** Jim gives Della combs. Now you know why he was so shocked to see Della's short hair.

**Plot:** It turns out that Jim sold his watch to buy Della the combs. This is a **surprise ending.** It is also an example of **irony.** Irony is present when what happens is the opposite of what you expect. Each person gives up a treasure to buy a gift. And the gift in both cases turns out to be useless.

**Theme:** The author tells you that Jim and Della are the Magi. The Magi gave gifts to show their love for Jesus. Jim and Della give gifts to show their love for each other. The gifts are not useful, but they show that Jim and Della's love is strong. This makes Jim and Della wiser than people who do not show their love.

brought Christmas gifts to the baby Jesus. But they could not give gifts like Jim's and Della's. Perhaps you don't understand me now. But you will understand soon.

Jim took a small box out of his pocket. "I love your short hair, Della," he said. "I'm sorry I seemed strange. But if you open the box, you will understand." Della opened the box. First she smiled, then suddenly she began to cry. In the box were two beautiful combs. Combs like those were made to hold up long hair. Della could see that the combs came from an expensive store. She never thought she would ever have anything as beautiful! "Oh, Jim, they are lovely! And my hair grows fast, you know. But wait! You must see your gift." Della gave Jim the chain. The chain was bright, like her eyes. "Isn't it a good one, Jim? I looked for it everywhere. You'll have to look at the time one hundred times daily, now. Give me your watch. I want to see them together."

Jim lay back on the couch. He put his hands under his head, and smiled. "Della," he said, "let's put the gifts away. They are too good for us right now. I sold the watch to buy your combs. Come on, let's have dinner."

The Magi, as we said, were wise men—very wise men. They brought gifts to the baby Jesus. The Magi were wise, so their gifts were wise gifts. Perhaps Jim and Della do not seem wise. They lost the two great treasures of their house. But I want to tell you that they were wise. People like Jim and Della are always wiser than others. Everywhere they are wiser. They are the Magi.

# 1

# Love of Life

***Adapted from the story by Jack London***

### *About the Author*

Jack London was born in San Francisco, California, in 1876. His family was poor. He left school at fourteen. He worked on boats, on farms, and in the woods. London loved to visit new places. His first long trip was to Japan. When London was eighteen, he returned to high school for one year. Then he went to the University of California at Berkeley. But, again, he left after one year and began to write. In 1897 London went to the Klondike, in northwestern Canada, near Alaska. Many people went there to find gold. London wrote stories about his experiences there. He traveled to many other places, too, and found adventures everywhere. He put these adventures into his famous stories and novels. London continued to travel until a few years before his death in 1916.

# Before You Read

## About "Love of Life"

**Characters**
The first man, who is not named; the other man, Bill; some sailors

**Plot**
A man has been looking for gold and is now far from his camp. He tries to find his way to a safe place where he can find the food and help he needs.

**Setting**
*Time:* the late 1890s
*Place:* the Klondike (northwestern Canada)

**Theme**
A person who has been hungry for a long time never forgets what hunger is.

## Build Background

### The Klondike Gold Rush

In 1897–1898, thousands of people went to the Klondike to find gold. The Klondike is an area in northwestern Canada, near Alaska. A few people did find gold. These lucky people became rich overnight. But most people found little or no gold.

The Klondike was a difficult place to live. Life was so hard that many people gave up and went home. Others died from cold, hunger, or disease.

Winter in the Klondike lasts seven months. But the mountains there are very beautiful. Would you like to go to the Klondike? Why or why not?

## Key Words

Read these sentences. Try to understand each word in dark type by looking at the other words in the sentence. Use a dictionary to check your ideas. Write each word and its meaning in your notebook.

| blanket |
| --- |
| bullets |
| camp |
| hunger |
| wolf |

1. The man put a **blanket** on his shoulders to keep warm.
2. There were no **bullets** in the gun, so the man could not shoot it.
3. At a **camp,** a traveler might stop to rest and get some food to eat.
4. The man's **hunger** made him look for food.
5. The man thought he saw a dog, but the animal was a **wolf.**

## Reading Strategy

### Predict

You will understand a text better if you **predict,** or guess, what will happen next. As you read, follow these steps:

- Stop reading from time to time. Ask yourself, "What will happen next?"
- Look for clues in the story and the pictures.
- Think about what you already know.
- Think about your own experiences.
- Then continue reading to see if your prediction is correct.

# Love of Life

***Adapted from the story by Jack London***

Two men walked slowly through the low water of a river. They were alone in the cold, empty land. All they could see were stones and earth. It was fall, and the river ran cold over their feet. They carried blankets on their backs. They had guns, but no bullets; matches, but no food.

"I wish we had just two of those bullets we hid in the camp," said the first of the men. His voice was tired. The other man did not answer.

Suddenly the first man fell over a stone. He hurt his foot badly, and he cried out. He lay still for a moment, and then called, "Hey, Bill, I've hurt my foot." Bill didn't stop or look back. He walked out of the river and over the hill. The other man watched him. His eyes seemed like the eyes of a sick animal. He stood up. "Bill!" he cried again. But there was no answer. Bill kept walking.

"Bill!"

The man was alone in the empty land. His hands were cold, and he dropped his gun. He fought with his fear, and took his gun out of the water. He followed slowly after Bill. He tried to walk lightly on his bad foot.

He was alone, but he was not lost. He knew the way to their camp. There he would find food, bullets, and blankets. He must find them soon. Bill would wait for him there. Together they would go south to the Hudson Bay Company. They would find food there, and a warm fire. Home. The man had to believe that Bill would wait for him at the camp. If not, he would die. He thought about the food in the camp. And the food at the Hudson Bay Company. And the food he ate two days ago. He thought about food and he walked. After a while the man found some small berries to eat. The berries had no taste, and did not fill him. But he knew he must eat them.

In the evening he hit his foot on a stone and fell down. He could not get up again. He lay still for a long time. Later, he felt a little better and got up. He made a fire. He could cook only hot water, but he felt warmer. He dried his shoes by the fire. They had many holes. His feet had blood on them. His foot hurt badly. He put his foot in a piece of his blanket. Then he slept like a dead man.

He woke up because he heard an animal near him. He thought of meat and took his gun. But he had no bullets. The animal ran away. The man stood up and cried out. His foot was much worse this morning. He took out a small bag that was in his blanket. It was heavy—fifteen pounds. He didn't know if he could carry it. But he couldn't leave it behind. He had to take it with him. He had to be strong enough. He put it into his blanket again.

That day his hunger grew worse, worse than the hurt in his foot. Many times he wanted to lie down, but hunger made him go on. He saw a few birds. Once he tried to catch one, but it flew away. He felt tired and sick. He forgot to follow the way to the camp. In the afternoon he found some green plants. He ate them fast, like a horse. He saw a small fish in a river. He tried to catch it with his cup. But the fish swam away into a hole. The man cried like a baby, first quietly, then loudly. He cried alone in that empty world.

That night he made a fire again, and drank hot water. His blanket was wet, and his foot hurt. He could think only of his hunger. He woke up cold and sick. The earth and sky were gray. He got up and walked, he didn't know where. But the small bag was with him. The sun came out again, and he saw that he was lost. Was he too far north? He turned toward the east. His hunger was not so great, but he knew he was sick. He stopped often. He heard wolves, and knew that deer were near him. He believed he had one more bullet in his gun. But it was still empty. The small bag became too heavy. The man opened the bag. It was full of small pieces of gold. He put half the gold in a piece of his blanket and left it on a rock. But he kept his gun. There were bullets in that camp.

Days passed, days of rain and cold. One day he came to the bones of a deer. There was no meat on the bones. The man knew wolves must be near. He broke the bones and ate like an animal. Would he, too, be only bones tomorrow? And why not? This was life, he thought. Only life hurt. There was no hurt in death. To die was to sleep. Then why was he not ready to die? He could not see or feel. The hunger, too, was gone. But he walked and walked.

One morning he woke up beside a river. Sunlight was warm on his face. A sunny day, he thought. Perhaps he could find his way to the camp. His eyes followed the river. He could see far. The river emptied into the sea. He saw a ship on that silver sea. He shut his eyes. He knew there could be no ship, no seas, in this land. He heard a noise behind him, and turned back. A wolf, old and sick, was following him. I know *this* is real, he thought. He turned again, but the sea and the ship were still there. He didn't understand it. He tried to remember. What did the men at the Hudson Bay Company say about this land? Was he walking north, away from the camp, toward the sea? The man moved slowly toward the ship. He knew the sick wolf was following him. In the afternoon, he found more bones left by wolves. The bones of a man! Beside the bones was a small bag of gold, like his own. Ha! Bill carried his gold to the end, he thought. He would take Bill's gold to the ship. He would have the last laugh on Bill. His laughing sounded like the low cry of an animal. The wolf cried back to the man, and the man stopped laughing. How could he laugh about Bill's bones? He could not take Bill's gold. He left the gold near the bones.

The man was very sick now. He walked more and more slowly. His blanket was gone. He lost his gold, then his gun, then his knife. Only the wolf stayed with him hour after hour. At last the man could go no further. He fell down. The wolf came close to him. It weakly bit his hand. The man hit the wolf and it went away. But it did not go far. It waited. The man waited. After many hours the wolf came back again. It was going to kill the man. But the man was ready. He held the wolf's mouth closed, and he got on top of the sick wolf. He

held the animal still. Then he bit it with his last strength. He tasted the wolf's blood in his mouth. Only love of life gave him enough strength. He held the wolf with his teeth and killed it. Later he fell on his back and slept.

The men on the ship saw a strange thing on the land. It did not walk. It was lying on the ground, and it moved slowly toward them—perhaps twenty feet an hour. The men went close to look at it. They could not believe it was a man.

Three weeks later the man felt better. He could tell them his story. But there was one strange thing. He could not believe there was enough food on the ship. The men told him there was a lot of food. But he only looked at them with fear. And slowly he began to grow fat. The men thought this was strange. They gave him less food, but still he grew larger and larger—each day he was fatter. Then one day they saw him put a lot of bread under his shirt. They looked in his bed, too, and saw bread under his blanket. The men understood, and left him alone.

# After You Read

## Understand the Story

Answer these questions in your notebook. Write complete sentences.

**1.** What did Bill do when the first man fell?

**2.** What was in the small bag that the man carried?

**3.** Why did the wolf follow the man?

**4.** How was the man saved?

**5.** Why did the man put bread under his shirt?

**6.** "Love of Life" is the title of the story. What does it mean? How does the man show that he loves life?

## Elements of Literature

### Setting

The **setting** is the time and place of a story. Read these sentences from "Love of Life." Then answer the question.

> Two men walked slowly through the low water of a river. They were alone in the cold, empty land. All they could see were stones and earth. It was fall, and the river ran cold over their feet.

Which words tell you about the story's time and place? Write these words in your notebook.

## Discussion

Discuss in pairs or small groups.

1. Why does the man laugh when he finds Bill's bag of gold? Why does he stop laughing? Why does the man leave the gold where he found it?
2. Why was the man not sure that the ship he saw was real?
3. Did the man have enough food to eat on the ship? Why was he still afraid of being hungry?

## Vocabulary

Choose the correct word. Write the completed sentences in your notebook.

1. The men had guns, but no ______.
   **a.** matches **b.** blankets **c.** bullets
2. The man put a piece of his ______ around his hurt foot.
   **a.** blanket **b.** shoe **c.** shirt
3. The man wanted to find his ______ because food and bullets were there.
   **a.** gold **b.** river **c.** camp
4. The man's ______ grew worse than the hurt in his foot.
   **a.** pain **b.** hunger **c.** anger
5. An old and sick ______ was following the man.
   **a.** wolf **b.** deer **c.** fish

## Word Study

**Adverbs** are words that tell you how something happens. Adverbs are often made by adding *-ly* to the adjective form of a word.

Write the sentences below in your notebook. Complete each sentence with the correct form of the word. Use the chart to help you. The first item has been done for you.

| Adjective | Adverb | Adjective | Adverb |
|---|---|---|---|
| slow | slowly | hungry | hungrily |
| sudden | suddenly | strange | strangely |
| tired | tiredly | light | lightly |
| weak | weakly | quiet | quietly |

1. The man walked very ___slowly___.
   **slow/slowly**

2. Bill wondered, "If I die ________________, what will happen to my gold?"
   **sudden/suddenly**

3. The man was hungry and ________________.
   **tired/tiredly**

4. The wolf was ________________, like the man.
   **weak/weakly**

5. The man ate the bones ________________.
   **hungry/hungrily**

6. The men on the ship saw a ________________ thing.
   **strange/strangely**

7. The man walked ________________ on his hurt foot.
   **light/lightly**

8. The man was ________________ as he tried to catch the fish.
   **quiet/quietly**

# Extension Activity

## Wolves

In the story "Love of Life," a sick wolf attacks the lost man. You may be surprised to learn that healthy wolves do not usually attack people.

**A.** Read more about wolves.

> Most wolves travel around in groups called packs. The leader of the pack is usually a male wolf. This wolf is called the alpha male. His mate is the alpha female. She is the only female in the pack that is allowed to have pups. All the wolves in a pack hunt together and help raise the young wolves.
>
> Wolves have very good eyesight. They also have strong senses of smell and hearing. A wolf can smell and see a deer from more than a mile away.

**B.** Work with a partner to make a poster about wolves. Follow the steps below.

1. Use the Internet or library books to find more information about wolves. Take notes.
2. Paste or draw a picture of a wolf on your poster.
3. Write some facts about wolves around the picture.

# Writing Practice

## Write Comparisons

In "Love of Life," the author uses the word *like* in comparisons that describe the man. Here are some examples:

> His eyes seemed like the eyes of a sick animal.
>
> . . . he slept like a dead man.
>
> He ate them fast, like a horse.
>
> His laughing sounded like the low cry of an animal.

Making comparisons—comparing one thing to another—is a way of making your writing more interesting.

Write six sentences of your own that have comparisons in them. Use the word *like* in your comparisons. Below are some examples you can use in your sentences. You may also make up your own.

**Comparisons with *like***

run like the wind

swim like a fish

spread like wildfire

cry like a baby

2

# A Cub-Pilot's Education

*Adapted from the story by Mark Twain*

## *About the Author*

Mark Twain's real name was Samuel Langhorne Clemens. He was born in 1835 in Missouri. As a boy, he lived in a small town on the Mississippi River. His most famous books, *The Adventures of Tom Sawyer* and *The Adventures of Huckleberry Finn,* are about boyhood and the Mississippi. These books made Mark Twain one of America's most famous and best-loved writers. He died in 1910 at the age of seventy-five. This story is from his book *Life on the Mississippi.*

# Before You Read

## About "A Cub-Pilot's Education"

**Characters**
The narrator, the boy who tells the story; Mr. Bixby, a steamboat pilot; Ben, the man in the engine room

**Plot**
More than anything, the narrator (storyteller) wants to become a steamboat pilot. He goes to New Orleans, where Mr. Bixby allows him to be a cub-pilot. Mr. Bixby teaches the narrator a lesson he will never forget.

**Setting**
*Time:* middle 1800s
*Place:* New Orleans, the Mississippi River

**Theme**
Trusting yourself is an important part of being a responsible person.

## Build Background

### Travel by Steamboat

Steamboats are boats powered by steam engines. In 1807, a man named Robert Fulton built a steamboat called the *Clermont*. The *Clermont* made a successful trip up the Hudson River from New York City to Albany, New York. Soon after, people began traveling and shipping goods on steamboats along America's rivers. The Mississippi River, especially, became an important route for steamboat transportation.

Imagine that you lived on the Mississippi River in the 1800s. Would you be excited when the steamboat came up or down the river? Why or why not?

## Key Words

Read these sentences. Try to understand each word in dark type by looking at the other words in the sentence. Use a dictionary to check your ideas. Write each word and its meaning in your notebook.

| |
|---|
| cub-pilot |
| landing |
| Mississippi River |
| mist |
| steamboat |

1. A person who wants to be steamboat pilot should first train as a **cub-pilot.**
2. The steamboat stopped at the **landing.** People were waiting there to unload goods from the boat.
3. The boy lived in a village on the **Mississippi River.** He liked living by the water because he loved to watch the steamboats.
4. The air was filled with tiny drops of water. This **mist** made it hard for the pilot to see where he was going.
5. The **steamboat** comes down the river. Steam engines make the big wheel turn, moving the boat forward.

## Reading Strategy

### Look for Causes and Effects

Looking for **causes and effects** as you read can help you better understand a story. Most stories tell about an event. Why an event happens is a cause. What happens—the event itself—is an effect. As you read, as yourself these questions:

- What is happening? That's an effect.
- Why is it happening? That's a cause.
- Which causes and effects lead from one to the other?

# A Cub-Pilot's Education

*Adapted from the story by Mark Twain*

## I

All the boys in my village wanted to be the same thing: a steamboat pilot. Our village lay on the great Mississippi River. Once a day, at noon, a steamboat came up from St. Louis. Later, at 1:00 o'clock, another came down from Keokuk. Before these hours, the day was full and bright with waiting. After them, the day was a dead and empty thing.

I can see that old time now. The white town sleeps in the morning sun. The streets are empty. Some animals walk near the buildings. The waters of the Mississippi are quiet and still. Men sit outside their stores in chairs. They look at the town and don't talk much.

Then a worker cries, "S-t-e-a-m-boat coming!" And everything changes! Suddenly the streets are full. Men, women, and children run to the steamboat landing. The animals make a hundred different noises. The town wakes up!

The steamboat which comes toward the town is long and pretty. Her big wheel turns and turns. Everybody looks at her and at the men who live on her. The pilot stands tallest, the center of everything, the king. Slowly the steamboat comes to the landing. Men take things off the boat and bring other things on. In ten minutes she is gone again. The town goes back to sleep. But the boys of the town remember the boat. They remember the pilot. And they don't forget.

I was fifteen then, and I ran away from home. I went to New Orleans. There I met a pilot named Mr. Bixby. I said I wanted to be his cub-pilot, or learner. He said no—but only once. I said yes a hundred times. So in the end I won. He said he would teach me the river. He didn't smile or laugh, but I was the happiest boy in the city.

We left New Orleans at four o'clock one afternoon. Mr. Bixby was at the wheel. Here at the beginning of the river, there were a lot of steamboats. Most of them were at landings on the sides of the river. We went past them quickly, very close to them. Suddenly Mr. Bixby said, "Here. You steer her." And he gave me the wheel. My heart was in my mouth. I thought it was very dangerous, close to those other boats. I began to steer into the middle of the river. In the middle, there was enough water for everybody.

"What are you doing?" Mr. Bixby cried angrily. He pushed me away and took the wheel again. And again he steered us near the other boats. After a while, he became a little cooler. He told me that water runs fast in the middle of a river. At the sides, it runs slow. "So if you're going up-river, you have to steer near the sides. You can go in the middle only if you're going down-river." Well, that was good enough for me. I decided to be a down-river pilot only.

Sometimes Mr. Bixby showed me points of land. "This is Six-Mile Point," he said. The land pointed like a finger into the water. Another time, he said, "This is Nine-Mile Point." It looked like Six-Mile Point to me. Later, he said, "This is Twelve-Mile Point." Well, this wasn't very interesting news. All the points seemed the same.

After six hours of this, we had supper and went to bed. Even bed was more interesting than the "points." At midnight, someone put a light in my eyes. "Hey, let's go!"

Then he left. I couldn't understand this. I decided to go back to sleep. Soon the man came again with his light; now he was angry. "Wake up!" he called. I was angry, too, and said, "Don't put that light in my eyes! How can I sleep if you wake me up every minute?"

All the men in the room laughed at this. The man left again, but came back soon with Mr. Bixby. One minute later I was climbing the steps to the pilot-house. Some of my clothes were on me. The rest were in my hands. Mr. Bixby walked behind me, angry. Now, here was something interesting: Pilots worked in the middle of the night!

And that night was a bad one. There was a lot of mist on the river. You could not see through it. Where were we going? I was frightened. But Mr. Bixby turned the wheel easily and happily. He told me we had to find a farm. Jones Farm. To myself I said, "Okay, Mr. Bixby. You can try all night. But you'll never find anything in this mist."

Suddenly Mr. Bixby turned to me and said, "What's the name of the first point above New Orleans?"

I answered very quickly. I said I didn't know.

"Don't *know*?"

The loudness of his voice surprised me. But I couldn't answer him.

"Well then," he said, "What's the name of the next point?"

Again I didn't know.

"Now, look! After Twelve-Mile Point, where do you cross the river?"

"I-I-I don't know."

"You-you-you don't know? Well, what *do* you know?"

"I—nothing, it seems."

"Nothing? *Less* than nothing! You say you want to pilot a steamboat on the river? My boy, you couldn't pilot a cow down a street! Why do you think I told you the names of those points?"

"Well, to-to—be interesting, I thought."

"What! To be *interesting*?" Now he was *very* angry. He walked across the pilot-house and back again. This cooled him down. "My boy," he said more softly, "You must get a little notebook. I will tell you many names of places on this river. You must write them all down. Then you must remember them. All of them. That is the only way to become a pilot."

My heart fell. I never remembered things easily in school. But also I didn't fully believe Mr. Bixby. No one, I thought, could know all of the Mississippi. No one could put that great river inside his head.

Then Mr. Bixby pulled a bell. A worker's voice came up from below.

"What's this, sir?

"Jones Farm," Mr. Bixby said.

I could see nothing through the mist. And Mr. Bixby could see nothing. I knew that. So I didn't believe him. How could I? We were in the middle of nowhere! But soon the boat's nose softly hit the landing. Worker's voices came up to us. I still couldn't believe it, but this was Jones Farm!

## II

And so, slowly, I began to put the Mississippi River inside my head. I filled a notebook—I filled two notebooks—with names from the river. Islands, towns, points, bends in the river. The names of all these things went into my notebooks. And slowly some of them began to go into my head. Then more of them. I began to feel better about myself. I was beginning to learn the river.

Then one day Mr. Bixby said to me, "What is the shape of Apple Bend?"

"The shape of Apple Bend?"

"Yes, of course."

"I know the *name* of Apple Bend. I know where it is. Don't tell me I have to know the shape of it, too!"

Mr. Bixby's mouth went off like a gun, bang! He shot all his bad words at me. Then, as always, he cooled. "My boy," he said, "you must learn the shape of this river and everything on it. If you don't know the shape, you can't steer at night. And of course, the river has two shapes. One during the day, and one at night."

"Oh, no!"

"Oh yes. Look: How can you walk through a room at home in the dark? Because you know the shape of it. You can't see it."

"You mean I must know this river like the rooms at home?"

"No. I mean you must know it *better* than the rooms at home."

"I want to die."

"My boy, I don't want you to be sad or angry. But there is more."

"All right. Tell me everything. Give it to me!"

I'm sorry, but you must learn these things. There is no other way. Now, a night with stars throws shadows. Dark shadows change the shape of the river. You think you are coming to a bend, but there is no bend. And this is different from a night with no stars. On a night with no stars, the river has a different shape. You think there are no bends, but there *are* bends. And of course, on a night with mist, the river has no shape. You think you are going to steer the boat onto land. But then suddenly you see that it's water, not land. Well. Then you have your moonlight nights. Different kinds of moonlight change the shape of the river again. And there are different kinds of shadows, too. Different shadows bring different shapes to the river. You see—"

"Oh, stop!" I cried. "You mean I have to learn the thousand million different shapes of this river?"

"No, no! You only learn *the* shape of the river. The *one* shape. And you steer by that. Don't you understand? You steer by the river that's in your head. Forget the one that's before your eyes."

"I see. And you think that's easy."

"I never said it was easy. And of course the river is always, always changing shape. The river of this week is different from the river of last week. And next week it will be different again."

"All right. Good-bye. I'm going home."

But of course I didn't go home, I stayed. I wanted to learn. I *needed* to learn. And day by day, month by month, I did learn. The river was my school. Slowly I began to think I was a good student. I could steer the boat alone, without Mr. Bixby's help. I knew the river like the room of my house—no, better. I could steer at night, by the shape of the river in my head. No cub-pilot was better, I thought. Oh, my nose was very high in the air!

Of course, Mr. Bixby saw this. And he decided to teach me another lesson.

One beautiful summer's day we were near the bend above Island 66. I had the wheel. We were in the middle of the river. It was easy water, deep and wide.

Mr. Bixby said, "I am going below for a while. Do you know how to run the next bend?"

A strange question! It was perhaps the easiest bend in the river. I knew it well. It began at a little island. The river was wide there, and more than a hundred feet deep. There was no possible danger.

"Know how to *run* it? Why, I can run it with my eyes closed!"

"How much water is there in it?"

"What kind of question is that? There's more water there than in the Atlantic Ocean."

"You think so, do you?"

He left, and soon I began to worry. There was something in his voice. . . .

I didn't know it, but Mr. Bixby had stayed close to the pilot-house. I couldn't see him, but he was talking to some of the men. Soon a worker came and stood in front of the pilot-house. He looked a little worried. We were near the island at the beginning of the bend. Another man came and stood with the first. He looked worried, too. Then another. They looked at me, then at the water, then at me again. Soon there were fifteen or twenty people out there in front of me. No one said anything. The noise of the engines suddenly seemed loud to me.

Then one of them said in a strange voice, "Where is Mr. Bixby?"

"Below," I said. The man turned away and said nothing more.

Now I became *very* worried. I steered a little to the right. I thought I saw danger! I steered to the left. More danger! I wanted to go slower. I wanted to stop the engines. I didn't know *what* I wanted.

In the end I called down to the engine room. "How deep is it here? Can you tell me soon? Please be quick!"

"Forty feet," came the voice. He had the answer already! Forty feet? It couldn't be! Why, the water there was as deep as . . .

"Thirty-five," he said in a worried voice. "Thirty-two! Twenty-eight!"

I couldn't believe it! I ran to the wheel, pulled a bell, stopped the engines.

"Eighteen!" came the voice. "Fifteen! Thirteen! Ten!"

Ten feet! I was filled with fear now. I did not know what to do. I called loudly down to the man in the engine room. "Back!" I called. "Please, Ben, back her! Back her! Oh, Ben, if you love me, back her now!"

I heard the door close softly. I looked around, and there stood Mr. Bixby. He smiled a sweet smile at me. Then all the people in front of the pilot-house began to laugh. I understood it all now, and I felt two feet tall. I started the engines again. I steered to the middle of the river without another word. After a while, I said, "That was kind and loving of you, wasn't it? I think I'll hear that story the rest of my life."

"Well, perhaps you will. And that won't be a bad thing. I want you to learn something from this. Didn't you *know* there was a hundred feet of water at that bend?"

"Yes, I did."

"All right, then. If you know a thing, you must believe it—and deeply. The river is in your head, remember? And another thing. If you get into a dangerous place, don't turn and run. That doesn't help. You must fight fear, always. And on the river there is always fear."

It was a good lesson, perhaps his best lesson. And I never forgot it. But I can tell you, it cost a lot to learn it. Every day for weeks and weeks I had to hear those difficult words: "Oh, Ben, if you love me, back her!"

# After You Read

## Understand the Story

Answer these questions in your notebook. Write complete sentences.

1. What kind of boat was Mr. Bixby the pilot of?
2. What was Mr. Bixby like? Describe his personality.
3. Why did Mr. Bixby get angry at the narrator the first time the boy steered the boat?
4. Why was it important for the narrator to learn the shape of the river?
5. What did Mr. Bixby do to confuse the narrator near the bend above Island 66?
6. Why did Mr. Bixby trick the narrator into thinking the river was not deep at that point?

## Elements of Literature

### Characterization

Read this passage from the story. Then answer the questions.

> Mr. Bixby's mouth went off like a gun, bang! He shot all his bad words at me. Then, as always, he cooled. "My boy," he said, "you must learn the shape of this river and everything on it. If you don't know the shape, you can't steer at night. And of course, the river has two shapes. One during the day, and one at night."

What does this passage tell you about Mr. Bixby? How can you tell that Mr. Bixby really cares about the narrator? Does the narrator become a good steamboat pilot? Explain.

## Discussion

Discuss in pairs or small groups.

**1.** Why does Mr. Bixby speak in a loud and angry voice throughout the story? Do you think Mr. Bixby is really angry with the boy? Explain your answer.

**2.** In "A Cub-Pilot's Education," the narrator learns the shape of the Mississippi River, so that he knows every point and bend. Is there a place that you know as well as the boy knows the river? Describe it.

## Vocabulary

Choose the correct word. Write the completed sentences in your notebook.

**1.** All the boys in my village wanted to be the same thing: a ______ pilot.
**a.** mist **b.** steamboat **c.** landing

**2.** The ______ is the second longest river in the United States.
**a.** Mississippi River **b.** Amazon River **c.** Nile River

**3.** I told Mr. Bixby I wanted to be his ______, or learner.
**a.** landing **b.** cub-pilot **c.** steamboat

**4.** The steamboat was at a ______ on the side of the river.
**a.** landing **b.** mist **c.** cub-pilot

**5.** You could not see through the ______ on the river.
**a.** cub-pilot **b.** Mississippi **c.** mist

## Word Study

Write the sentences in your notebook. Complete each sentence with the correct form of the word. Use the chart to help you. The first one is done for you.

| Adjective | Adverb |
|---|---|
| angry | angrily |
| quiet | quietly |
| sleepy | sleepily |
| soft | softly |
| slow | slowly |
| different | differently |

1. "What are you doing?" Mr. Bixby cried angrily.
   **angry/angrily**
2. The waters of the Mississippi River were ________ and still.
   **quiet/quietly**
3. The boy walked ________ to the pilot-house.
   **sleepy/sleepily**
4. The boat's nose ________ hit the landing.
   **soft/softly**
5. The boy was not a ________ learner.
   **slow/slowly**
6. The river can have several ________ shapes.
   **different/differently**

# Extension Activity

## More about Steamboat Travel

In "A Cub-Pilot's Education," you read about traveling by steamboat on the Mississippi River. Steamboat travel was important in the history of the United States.

**A.** Read more about steamboats.

In the 1800s, steamboat travel became part of American life. At that time steamboats were the best—and often the only—way to travel or to carry things. Businesses used steamboats to deliver their goods. People were able to get to more places than ever before. The Mississippi River and the rivers that connect to it offered many routes to different places. Steamboats helped to change where people lived in the United States—many people traveled west on steamboats. In time, however, train travel replaced steamboat travel because it was faster and easier.

**B.** Design a travel brochure (a small paper book of 5–6 pages with pictures and descriptions). Your brochure will advertise a steamboat trip along the Mississippi River. Describe the special sights and sounds people will enjoy as they ride up and down "Old Man River." Include pictures in your brochure.

# Writing Practice

## Write a Journal Entry

Sometimes people record their thoughts and feelings about things by writing in a **journal.** Each piece of writing in a journal is called an **entry.** A journal can help a person remember important events. A journal entry may begin with a date or words that mark the time.

Imagine that the narrator of the story kept a journal. An entry describing his first day might have been something like this:

My First Day

My first day as a cub-pilot began as we left New Orleans. It was exciting to watch Mr. Bixby steer the boat. He was careful as he passed other boats. We were very close to them. I was shocked by what he did next. He made me take the wheel! I was terribly frightened, but tried not to show it. The first thing I did was steer the boat toward the middle of the river. I wanted badly to get away from the other boats. What a huge mistake! Mr. Bixby grabbed the wheel away from me. He told me that the water runs fast in the middle of the river—too fast for going up-river. He told me to stay near the sides. I guess I have a lot to learn.

Write a journal entry of your own. Tell about something that happened to you yesterday or today. Describe what happened and your feelings about it. Remember that this journal is not private. Include only things you would want another person to read.

# The Tell-Tale Heart

***Adapted from the story by Edgar Allan Poe***

## *About the Author*

Edgar Allan Poe was born in 1809 in Boston, Massachusetts. His parents died when he was a small child. He lived with the Allan family. They moved to England when Poe was six. Poe often fought with Mr. Allan and separated from him at the age of twenty-two.

Allan had become very rich, but Poe was poor for the rest of his life. He worked for magazines but lost many jobs. He married his young cousin, Virginia, but she became sick and died. Through all his difficulties, Poe never stopped writing, and his writing took many forms. He often wrote about the dark side of the human heart. People remember Poe now for his poetry and for his dark, strange stories like "The Tell-Tale Heart." Poe died at the age of forty in 1849.

# Before You Read

## About "The Tell-Tale Heart"

**Characters**
The narrator, probably a young man; an old man; three policemen

**Plot**
The narrator relives eight strange days by telling how and why he did a terrible thing. The story may be true. Or perhaps the narrator's anger made him imagine what he says happened. The narrator may have been evil (very bad) or out of his mind. Poe leaves that part of the plot for the reader to think about.

**Setting**
*Time:* about 1830
*Place:* the old man's house

**Theme**
Anger and fear can have great power over a person.

## Build Background

### Horror Stories

There were no horror movies, television shows, or radio shows when Edgar Allan Poe wrote his stories. People read books and magazines for entertainment. People who read Poe's stories enjoyed being scared by them. Since that time, many of Poe's stories have been made into movies and television shows. Now people can enjoy these stories both in print and on a screen.

Have you read a book or watched a movie that scared you? If so, describe the story. What was scary about it?

## Key Words

Read these sentences. Try to understand each word in dark type by looking at the other words in the sentence. Use a dictionary to check your ideas. Write each word and its meaning in your notebook.

| careful |
| --- |
| horrible |
| mad |
| nervous |

1. As the narrator begins the story, he repeats over and over how **careful** he was. He acted with care and planned everything he did.
2. The old man's strange eye frightened the young man. It was **horrible** to him. He couldn't look at it.
3. The horrible eye drove the young man **mad.** It made him lose his mind.
4. The young man was full of troubled thoughts. He was so **nervous** that he could not sleep.

## Reading Strategy

### Understand an Author's Purpose

Authors write fiction for different **purposes,** or reasons. Sometimes an author's purpose is to entertain the reader. Sometimes an author wants to teach the reader. Authors of horror stories like to scare their readers. Authors can have more than one purpose.

- As you read "The Tell-Tale Heart," look for words that show the author's purpose.
- What do you think was Poe's purpose for writing this story? Explain your answer.

# The Tell-Tale Heart

***Adapted from the story by Edgar Allan Poe***

True! Nervous. I was nervous then and I am nervous now. But why do you say that I am mad? Nothing was wrong with me. I could see very well. I could smell. I could touch. Yes, my friend, and I could hear. I could hear all things in the skies and in the earth. So why do you think that I am mad? Listen. I will tell you the story. I will speak quietly. You will understand everything. Listen!

Why did I want to kill the old man? Ah, this is very difficult. I liked the old man. No, I loved him! He never hurt me. He was always kind to me. I didn't need his gold; no, I didn't want that. I think it was his eye—yes, it was this! He had the eye of a bird. It was a cold, light-blue eye—a horrible eye. I feared it. Sometimes I tried to look at it. But then my blood ran cold. So, after many weeks, I knew I must kill the old man. His horrible eye must not live. Do you understand?

Now here is the point. You think that I am mad. Madmen know nothing. But I? I was careful. Oh, I was very careful. *Careful*, you see? For one long week, I was very kind to the old man. But every night, at midnight, I opened his door slowly, carefully. I had a lantern with me. Inside the lantern there was a light. But the sides of the lantern hid the light. So, first I put the dark lantern through the open door. Then I put my head in the room. I put it in slowly, very slowly. I didn't want to wake the old man. Ha! Would a madman be careful, like that? There was no noise, not a sound. I opened the lantern carefully—very carefully—and slowly. A thin light fell upon the old man's eye. I held it there. I held it there for a long time. And I did this every night for seven nights. But always the eye was closed. And so I could not do my work. I was not angry at the old man, you see. I was angry only at his horrible eye. And every morning I went into his room happily. I was friendly with him. I asked about his night. Did he sleep well? Was he all right? And so, you see, he knew nothing.

On the eighth night, I was more careful than before. I know you don't believe me, but it is true. The clock's hand moved more quickly than my hand. I opened the door slowly. I put the lantern in the room. The old man moved suddenly in his bed. But I did not go back. The room was very dark. I knew he could not see me. I put my head in the room. I began to open the lantern, but my hand hit the side. It made a loud noise.

The old man sat up quickly in bed. "Who's there?" he cried.

I stood still and said nothing. For one long hour I did not move a finger. And he did not lie down. He sat in his bed. He listened. I knew his fear!

And soon I heard another sound. It came from the old man. It was a horrible sound, the sound of fear! I knew that sound well. Often, at night, I too have made that sound. What was in the room? The old man didn't know. He didn't want to know. But he knew that he was in danger. Ah, yes, he knew!

And now I began to open the lantern. I opened it just a little. A small thin light fell upon the horrible blue eye.

It was open—wide, wide open. I could not see the old man's face or body. But I saw the eye very well. The horrible bird's eye. My blood ran cold. At the same time, anger began to grow inside me.

And now, haven't I told you that I could hear everything? Now a low, quick sound came to my ears. It was like the sound of a small wooden clock. I knew *that* sound well, too. It was the beating of the old man's heart!

My fear and anger grew. But I did not move. I stood still. I held the light on the old man's eye. And the beating of the heart grew. It became quicker and quicker, and louder and louder every second! I knew that his fear was very great. *Louder,* do you hear? I have told you that I am nervous. And this is true. My fear was like the old man's. But I did not move. I held the light on his eye. But the beating

grew louder, LOUDER! And now a new fear came to me. Someone in the next house would hear! The old man must die! This was his hour! With a loud cry, I opened the lantern wide. I ran into the room! The old man cried loudly once—once only. His fear, his fear killed him! In a second I pulled him from the bed. He lay still. I smiled a little. Everything was all right. For some minutes, I heard his heart beat softly. Then it stopped. I put my hand on his body. He was cold. He was like a stone. The old man was dead. His eye would never look upon me again!

And now I was very, very careful. I worked quickly but quietly. I used a good, new knife. I cut off the old man's arms and legs and head. Then I took three boards from the floor of the room. I put everything below the floor. Then I put the boards in their place again. I cleaned the floor. There was no blood. Nothing was wrong. I was *careful*, you see? Ha! Can you still think that I am mad?

I finished. It was four o'clock—still dark as midnight. Suddenly there was a beating on the door. Someone was there. But I went down with a happy heart. I had nothing to fear. Nothing.

Three policemen came into the house. They said that someone in the next house heard a cry. Was something wrong? Was everyone all right?

"Of course," I said. "Please come in." I was not nervous. I smiled at the men. I told them that the old man was in another town. I said he was with his sister. I showed them his money, his gold. Everything was there, in its place.

I brought chairs. I asked the men to sit. I sat, too. I sat on the boards over the dead man's body! I talked easily. The policemen smiled.

But after some minutes I became tired. Perhaps I was a little nervous. There was a low sound in my head, in my ears. I didn't like it. I talked more loudly, more angrily. Then suddenly I understood. The sound was not in my head or in my ears. It was there in the room!

Now I know that I became very nervous. *It was a low, quick sound. It sounded like a small wooden clock!* My eyes opened wide.

Could the policemen hear it? I talked in a louder voice. But the noise did not stop. It grew! I stood up and talked angrily, dangerously. I walked across the floor and back again. Why wouldn't the men leave? There was a storm inside my head! And still the noise became louder—LOUDER—LOUDER! I beat my hands on the table. I said dangerous things in a loud voice. But still the men talked happily and smiled. Couldn't they hear? Was it possible? Oh, God! No, no! They heard! They knew! They laughed at my hopes, and smiled at my fears. I knew it then and I know it now. I couldn't keep still! Anything was better than their smiles and laughing! And now—again!—listen! louder! LOUDER! LOUDER!

"Stop!" I cried. "Enough! Enough! Pull up the boards! Below the floor! Here, here!—It is the beating of his horrible heart!"

# After You Read

## Understand the Story

Answer these questions in your notebook. Write complete sentences.

1. At what time each night did the narrator visit the old man?
2. Why did the narrator want to kill the old man?
3. Why was the narrator friendly to the old man each morning?
4. Where did the narrator hide the old man's body?
5. Why did the policemen come to the house?
6. Why did the narrator make his voice louder and louder when he spoke to the policemen?

## Elements of Literature

### Foreshadowing

**Foreshadowing** is using clues to suggest events that have not yet happened. Read this passage from the story. Then answer the questions that follow it.

> And now, haven't I told you that I could hear everything? Now a low, quick sound came to my ears. It was like the sound of a small wooden clock. I knew *that* sound well, too. It was the beating of the old man's heart!

How does this passage give the reader a hint about how the story will end? Where else in the story does the author use the phrases "low, quick sound" and "small wooden clock"?

## Discussion

Discuss in pairs or small groups.

1. The old man was dead. His body, in pieces, was below the floor. But the narrator believed that he could hear the old man's heart beating. Why?

2. What do you think should happen to the narrator after the policemen take him away? Where does the narrator belong—in a prison or in a hospital?

3. Were you afraid while you read "The Tell-Tale Heart"? This kind of story is called a horror story. Do you enjoy horror stories? Why or why not?

## Vocabulary

Choose the correct word. Write the completed sentences in your notebook.

1. It was a cold, light-blue eye—a ______ eye.
   **a.** loud **b.** horrible **c.** careful

2. Every night, I opened his door slowly and ______.
   **a.** mad **b.** nervous **c.** carefully

3. I was not ______ when the three policemen came into the house.
   **a.** nervous **b.** heart **c.** horrible

4. I have not lost my mind, so why do you think that I am ______?
   **a.** careful **b.** mad **c.** lantern

## Word Study

Sometimes the noun form of a word is very different from the adjective and adverb forms. Look at the examples in the chart.

Write the sentences below in your notebook. Complete each sentence with the correct form of the word. Use the chart to help you. The first item has been done for you.

| Noun | Adjective | Adverb |
|---|---|---|
| horror | horrible | horribly |
| care | careful | carefully |
| danger | dangerous | dangerously |
| nerve | nervous | nervously |
| anger | angry | angrily |

1. The old man's eye seemed horrible to the young man. (**horror/horrible**)
2. The old man's eye filled the young man with ________. (**horror/horrible**)
3. The young man took ________ not to make a sound. (**care/careful**)
4. The policemen thought the young man might be ________. (**danger/dangerous**)
5. The young man's ________ were highly excited. (**nerves/nervous**)
6. The young man spoke more and more ________. (**nerves/nervously**)
7. The young man's fear and ________ grew. (**anger/angrily**)
8. He stood up and talked ________. (**angry/angrily**)

# Extension Activity

## Be a Critic

When a new book or movie comes out, people review it. They describe the book or movie and give it a rating, or say whether it is good or bad. People who review things are called reviewers or critics. A good critic does not give away the ending of a story.

**A.** Read this review by a critic who liked "The Tell-Tale Heart."

> "The Tell-Tale Heart" is a scary, fast-moving story. It takes place long ago. It is about a young man who is living in an old man's house. Suddenly, the young man kills the old man. The author gives you a lot of minute-to-minute details. But he leaves you with a lot of questions about why the young man behaves as he does. If you want a four-star reading adventure, get a copy of this story.

**B.** Be a movie critic. Share your review with a classmate.

- Write the name of the movie you saw.
- Tell who the main characters are.
- Describe the setting.
- Tell what happens to the main characters. Do not give away the ending.
- Rate the movie.

**Rating Chart**

| | |
|---|---|
| ★★★★ | = excellent |
| ★★★ | = good |
| ★★ | = okay |
| ★ | = not good |

# Writing Practice

## Write Interview Questions

In the story "The Tell-Tale Heart," the policemen **interview,** or question, the man. They interview him to find information. Here are some of the questions they may have asked:

- Who lives in this house?
- When was the last time you saw the old man?
- Did you and the old man get along well?

Good interviewers ask important questions. Good interviewers ask the kinds of questions that will get the information they need.

Plan an interview with your favorite author. Think about what you would like to know. Write a list of questions that you would ask the author. You might begin your list with these questions:

**1.** When did you first begin to write?

**2.** What was your first successful book?

# Of the Coming of John

***Adapted from the story by W. E. B. Du Bois***

## *About the Author*

W. E. B. Du Bois (pronounced Doo-BOYZ) was born in 1868 in Great Barrington, Massachusetts. He went to Fisk University, a college for black students in Nashville, Tennessee. There he learned that the problem of racial prejudice—judging people by the color of their skin—was worse in the South than it was in the North. Du Bois went on to become the first African American to earn a Ph.D. from Harvard University. Du Bois became a leader in the fight for racial equality in the United States. He helped begin the NAACP (National Association for the Advancement of Colored People). When Du Bois was ninety-three, he moved to Ghana, a country in Africa. He died in 1963. The story "Of the Coming of John" is from his most famous book, *The Souls of Black Folk* (1903).

# Before You Read

## About "Of the Coming of John"

**Characters**
John Jones, a young African American; the Judge, a powerful white man in the town; John, the Judge's son; Jennie, John Jones's younger sister

**Plot**
John Jones is sent North to get an education. He finds school and life in the North very difficult. When he returns home, his life is changed forever.

**Setting**
*Time:* the early 1900s
*Place:* Altamaha, Georgia

**Theme**
It is wrong to separate people because of their color.

## Build Background

### Civil Rights

Before the 1950s in the United States, people did not all have the same legal rights. In some states, there were laws about where African American people could go and where they could not go. In most southern states, there were separate schools for white children and for African American children. In 1954, in a court decision, *Brown v the Board of Education,* the Supreme Court ruled that is it not legal to separate public school students on the basis of color.

In this story, the term "color line" is used to describe the separation of black and white people. Some people believe that a kind of color line still exists today. What do you think?

## Key Words

Read these sentences. Try to understand each word in dark type by looking at the other words in the sentence. Use a dictionary to check your ideas. Write each word and its meaning in your notebook.

ghost
judge
proud
respect
respectful
spoil

1. I walked into a room full of people. But I felt like a **ghost** because no one spoke to me.
2. The **judge** listens to cases in a court. He or she decides what will happen to people who break the law.
3. The people were **proud** of John because he went to college.
4. We **respect** a person who is both good and successful.
5. We are **respectful** of a person who is both good and successful.
6. Some people think that giving too many gifts to children will **spoil** them, or make the children hard to manage.

## Reading Strategy

### Make Inferences

**Making inferences**, or **inferring**, is making reasonable guesses based on clues from the story. Read this passage from "Of the Coming of John":

> ". . . I knew your father, John. He belonged to my brother. He was a good black. Will you be like him? Or will you try to put foolish ideas in people's heads? Will you spoil them by making them think they are equal to whites?"
>
> "I know how things are here," John quickly answered.

The person talking to John does not think of John as an equal. You can infer that John understands this when he says, "I know how things are here."

Use clues from the story to make other inferences as you read.

# Of the Coming of John

*Adapted from the story by W. E. B. Du Bois*

## I

The bell rings at Wells Institute, and the students come in for supper. Tall and black, they move slowly, like ghosts against the light of sunset. Perhaps they *are* ghosts here. For this is a college for black students outside of a white city. The students almost never go into the city. The students almost don't exist for the whites.

Every evening, there is one student who always runs in late. The other students laugh as John hurries in after the bell. At first, his teachers excuse his lateness. He is a tall, thin brown boy. He seems to be growing out of his clothes. He is young and thoughtless. But he has a nice smile. He seems happy with the world.

John Jones came to Wells Institute from Altamaha in southeastern Georgia. The white people of Altamaha thought John was a good boy. He was a good farm worker. And he was always smiling and respectful. But they shook their heads in wonder when his mother sent him North to college. The white mailman said what most of the white people thought. "It will spoil him—destroy him," he said seriously. And he spoke as if he knew.

But on the day John left for college, half the black folk in town followed him to the train. They were so proud of him. The girls kissed him good-bye. The boys laughed and shook his hand. The train whistled. It was time to go. He kissed his little sister. He threw his long arms around his mother. The train whistled again, and carried him north, through the fields and farms, to Wells Institute.

John was their friend, brother, and son. After he left, his people kept saying proudly, "When John comes . . ." So many things would happen when John came home. Parties, speaking in church. John would learn to be a teacher, and there would be a new schoolhouse.

They had so many hopes for how John would help them. "When John comes . . ." But the white people wondered. They shook their heads. "School will spoil him."

At first, John was going to come home at Christmas. But the vacation was too short. Then for the summer. But his mother was poor, and the school cost a lot. So he worked at the Institute instead. Time went by, and two years passed. John's friends grew up, and his mother grew gray. His little sister, Jennie, went to work in a white man's kitchen. This man was a judge, rich and important.

Up at the Judge's house, the white people liked to hear the blacks say, "When John comes . . ." The Judge and his wife had a son named John, too. Their son John was tall and blond. When they were little, the two Johns had sometimes played together. Now he was away at college, too. At Princeton University. His parents were very proud of him. "He'll show those Northerners what a Southern gentleman can do!" the Judge would say proudly. And then he would say to Jennie, "How's *your* John? Too bad your mother sent him away to school. It will spoil him." He shook his head. Jennie listened to him respectfully. And she wondered.

## II

Up at Wells Institute, John's teachers were seriously worried about him. He was loud and noisy, always laughing and singing. He didn't know how to study. He seemed bored by books, and his schoolwork was careless. He was always late for everything. One night his teachers met to discuss him. They decided "that John Jones, because of continual lateness and careless work, must leave Wells Institute." Now John understood for the first time that school was really important. He understood at last that his noise and carelessness and continual lateness had gotten him into serious trouble with his teachers.

"But don't tell Mammy—you won't write to my mother, will you?" he said. "If you don't tell her, I'll go into the city and work.

And I'll come back next fall and show you something." His teachers liked him. They wanted to help him. They agreed that he could come back in the fall and try again.

It seemed to his teachers that John's face was always serious after that. When he returned to the Institute he began to respect his education, and he worked hard. He grew in body as well as mind. Slowly his clothes began to fit him better. His shirts were clean and his shoes were shiny. As the days passed he became more thoughtful. His teachers began to see that this careless boy was becoming a serious man.

Now John began to look at the world around him. He began to notice the difference between the lives of blacks and whites. He became angry when whites spoke to him without respect. Because he felt like a ghost in their world, he spent long hours worrying about the color line.

At last the day came when John finished Wells Institute. It was time to go back to Altamaha. He had always planned to work there after college. But now he wondered about living in that small town. Altamaha was deep in the South. Life wasn't easy for colored folk in the North, but it was even harder in the South. John knew he had to go back home. But he needed to take some time for himself first. So he decided to visit New York City first. "A breath of northern air before I go down South," he told himself.

## III

It was a bright morning in September. John sat watching the people walk by on the New York streets. He looked at all the rich clothes, the fashionable hats. "This is the big world, the *real* world," he thought.

He saw a lot of people going into a grand building. He was interested, and wondered what they were going to see. When he saw a tall blond man and a fashionably dressed woman go inside, he decided to follow.

Inside, John found himself in a line to buy tickets. He wasn't sure what to do. He had very little money. But he pulled out a five-dollar bill he had carefully saved. He was very surprised when he got no change back. How could he spend so much money on—what?

John began to hear soft voices behind him. "Be careful," he heard a woman say. She seemed to be joking with the man beside her. "You mustn't get angry just because a black man is in front of you in line."

"You don't understand us Southerners," said the blond man beside her. "You say there's no color line in the North. But we're more friendly to colored folk than you are. Why, my best friend when I was a boy was black. He was named John after me. We're friendly, but we don't spoil them, there."

They all sat down in the large music hall. In front of them, musicians and singers were ready to begin. The blond man looked angry when he saw that John was sitting beside them. But John didn't notice. He was too busy looking around. The inside of the building was beautiful. This was a world so different from his! Then the singing began. John felt that he was in a dream. He closed his eyes. The beautiful music rose up in the air. He wanted so much to rise up with it. He wanted to leave his low life. To fly like a bird in the free, sweet air. To live with pride in a world of beauty, and to feel that others respected him. As John sat forward to listen, his arm touched the lady next to him. The blond man noticed, and his face grew red. He lifted his arm to call someone.

John was completely lost in the music. At first he didn't hear the usher.

"Please come with me, sir," the usher said softly. John was surprised. As he stood up, he saw the angry face of the blond man for the first time. The man recognized John. And John saw that the man was the Judge's son.

"I'm sorry sir," the usher said when they had left the music hall. "We gave you the wrong seat. That seat was already sold. I am so sorry. Of course, we will give you back your money . . ."

But John turned and walked out of the building. "You're such a fool, John," he said, now angry at himself. He walked to his hotel and wrote a letter. "Dear mother and sister—I am coming—John."

## IV

Down in Altamaha, all the world knew John was coming. Most of the black folk came to meet his train. They were proud and excited. "John's coming!" they called to each other. They talked about the party for John at the church that night. They laughed and listened for the whistle of the train.

But John felt unhappy as he got off the train and looked around him. He was already angry because he had to ride South in a train car for blacks only. Now, the small, dirty town, the colorful, dirty faces of his people, made him sad. He had little to say to the happy group who came to welcome him. And the people quickly began to wonder about him. Was this cold, silent man their John? They had waited so long for him to come. Where was his smile, his laughter, his friendly handshake?

"He seems rather serious," said the minister of the church. "Or too proud for us?" his neighbor wondered. But the white mailman, passing by, said, "That fool black boy went North and got full of foolish ideas. But they won't work in Altamaha." The other whites agreed.

The welcome-home party at the church that night was a failure. Rain spoiled the barbeque. The ice cream melted. John was still cold and silent, and people didn't understand what was wrong. Then it was time for John to speak. He told his people that the world was changing. He spoke about the need for blacks to work to change the color line. More schools were needed, and better jobs. Blacks needed to forget their differences. They needed to work together to make better lives.

When he finished, the church was silent. People looked at each other in surprise. They didn't understand John. He had changed. He was not the boy they had known. He had become different from them.

John walked quietly out of the church. He stood alone in the darkness. His sister Jennie followed him.

"John," she said softly, "does it make everyone unhappy when they study and learn lots of things?"

He smiled at her. "I'm afraid it does," he said.

"And John, are you glad you studied?"

"Yes," he answered slowly. But he sounded sure of himself.

Jennie said thoughtfully, "I wish I was unhappy, John. And—and—I think I *am* a little unhappy." She put her arms around him.

A few days later, John went up to the Judge's house. He wanted to ask if he could become the teacher at the school for black children.

The Judge met him at the front door. "Go around to the back door and wait, John," he said. His face was unfriendly.

John sat on the kitchen stairs and waited. "I keep making mistakes," he said to himself. "Everything I do is wrong. I came home to help my people. But even before I left the train station, I hurt their feelings. I wanted to teach them what I think about the color line, and they don't understand. I told myself to show respect to the Judge. But then I go to his front door. I should know better!"

Just then Jennie opened the kitchen door. She said the Judge would see him now. When he went in, the Judge didn't ask him to sit down. Right away, he said, "You want to teach school, I suppose. Well, John, I want to tell you something. You know I am a friend of your people. I've helped your family. I would have helped you more if you hadn't gone away North. Now, I like you colored people. But you and I both know that in this country black people can't be equal to whites. You can be good and respectful workers. And I will try to help you. But the question is—will you teach your people to be good workers, like their mothers and fathers are? I knew your father, John. He belonged to my brother. He was a good black. Will you be like him? Or will you try to put foolish ideas in people's heads? Will you spoil them by making them think they are equal to whites?"

"I know how things are here," John quickly answered. But the Judge looked at him, and wondered.

## V

A month after John opened the school for black children, the Judge's son came home. This other John was tall and blond and sure of himself. His family was so proud of him. The whole white town was glad to see him come home. But things did not go well between John and his father. The Judge wanted his son to stay in Altamaha. He hoped his son would be a leader in town, like himself. But John thought the town was small and uninteresting—very boring, in fact. "Nothing here but dirt and blacks," he would say. "What could be more boring than that?" And he and the Judge would argue about it.

One evening when they were arguing about John's future, the mailman came to visit.

"I hear John's getting everybody excited over at the black school," he said.

"What do you mean?" asked the Judge.

"Oh, nothing much. Just, he talks to them about respect, and equality. About not saying 'sir' to a white man. Things like that."

"Who is this John?" asked the Judge's son.

"Why, it's little black John. You used to play with him," answered the Judge.

John looked angry, but then he laughed. "Oh," he said, "I saw him in New York. That's the black man that tried to push in and sit next to the lady I was with. . . ."

But the Judge had heard enough. All day, he had been feeling angry with his own John. Now it was time to do something about the other John. He went right to the schoolhouse door.

"John!" the Judge called out. His face was red with anger. "This school is closed. You children, go home and get to work. The white people of Altamaha are not spending their money on colored people just to fill their heads with foolish ideas! Go home! I'll close the door myself!"

Back at the Judge's house, his son looked around for something to do. He was bored with everything. His father's books were old, the town newspaper was foolish. He tried to sleep, but it was too hot. Finally, he walked out into the fields. "I feel like I'm in prison," he thought to himself. John wasn't really a bad young man. Just a little spoiled. And he was so sure of himself, like his proud father. "There isn't even a pretty girl around here," he said angrily.

Just then, he saw Jennie coming down the road. "I never noticed what a pretty girl she is!" he said to himself. "Hello, Jennie," he called out to her. "You haven't even given me a kiss since I came home!"

Jennie looked at him with surprise. She smiled respectfully and tried to pass by. But John was bored, and felt like playing with her. He took her arm. She was afraid, and turned and ran away. John ran after her.

Jennie's brother John was coming down the road. His heart was sad, and his thoughts were angry. "I can't live here anymore," he was thinking. "I'll go North and find work. I'll bring Mother and Jennie with me." He had never been so unhappy.

Suddenly he saw his sister in front of him. He heard her cry out in fear. John could see she was trying to escape from the arms of the tall, blond man. Without thinking, John picked up a tree branch. He hit the Judge's son hard, on the head. The young man fell down. His face was covered with blood.

John walked slowly home. "Mammy, I'm going away," he said. "I'm going to be free."

"Are you going North, son? Are you going North again?"

"Yes, Mammy, I'm going . . . North."

John walked slowly back down the road to wait for the white men. He saw blood on the ground where John's white body had fallen. They had played together as boys. He wondered where those little boys had gone. He thought about his life in the North. He seemed to hear again the singing from the beautiful music hall. Listen! But maybe it was only the men coming to get him. As he waited and listened, the sound became louder and louder, like a storm coming. He saw the old Judge, leading the other men. His face was white, his eyes red with anger. John felt sorry for him—so sorry. Then the men reached him, and the storm broke all around him.

And the world whistled in his ears.

# After You Read

## Understand the Story

Answer these questions in your notebook. Write complete sentences.

1. In what way were the students at Wells Institute "like ghosts"?
2. What did the white people of John's town think about his going North to college?
3. Why did John's teachers tell him he had to leave Wells Institute?
4. What did the usher in the music hall say to John about his seat? Was it true? Explain.
5. How did the judge feel about John wanting to teach in the school for black children?
6. Why did John say to his mother, "Yes, Mammy, I'm going . . . North"?

## Elements of Literature

### Theme

The **theme** is the central idea or message in a story. Read this passage from the story. Then answer the question.

> "John!" the Judge called out. His face was red with anger. "This school is closed. You children, go home and get to work. The white people of Altamaha are not spending their money on colored people just to fill their heads with foolish ideas! Go home! I'll close the door myself!"

The theme of this story is "It is wrong to separate people because of their color." How does this paragraph support the story's theme?

## Discussion

Discuss in pairs or small groups.

**1.** What does the final sentence of the story mean? What happens to John at the end of the story? How do you think life will be different for the black people of Altamaha after this?

**2.** Do you think John's mother was right to send him away to college? Why or why not?

## Vocabulary

Choose the correct word. Write the completed sentences in your notebook.

**1.** Tall and black, the students moved slowly, like ______ against the light of sunset.

**a.** judges **b.** ghosts **c.** proud

**2.** John's friends were so ______ of him on the day he left for college.

**a.** spoiled **b.** respect **c.** proud

**3.** Jennie worked for a ______ who was rich and important.

**a.** judge **b.** ghost **c.** mailman

**4.** When John returned to college, he began to ______ his education. He began to work hard at his studies.

**a.** proud **b.** spoil **c.** respect

**5.** Many white people in the town thought that school would ______ the black children.

**a.** spoil **b.** respect **c.** judge

**6.** Jennie was always ______ of the judge and his son.

**a.** respectful **b.** bored **c.** spoiled

## Word Study

Write the sentences below in your notebook. Complete each sentence with the correct form of the word. Use the chart to help you. The first item has been done for you.

| Verb | Noun | Adjective | Adverb |
| --- | --- | --- | --- |
| fail | failure | failed | failing |
| respect | respect | respectful | respectfully |
| fool | fool | foolish | foolishly |
| bore | boredom | boring | boringly |
| spoil | spoilage | spoiled | |

1. The welcome-home party at the church was a failure.
   **fail/failure**

2. John hoped that people would treat him with ________.
   **respect/respectful**

3. Jennie did not agree with what the Judge said about her brother John. But she listened to him ________ anyway.
   **respectful/respectfully**

4. Later, John thought he had been ________ to think white people would treat him well.
   **fool/foolish**

5. The Judge's son thought that Altamaha was ________.
   **boredom/boring**

6. The Judge's son was a ________ young man.
   **spoil/spoiled**

7. The white people of Altamaha believed that education would ________ the black people of the town.
   **spoil/spoilage**

# Extension Activity

## Learn More about Civil Rights

In "Of the Coming of John," there was much discrimination in the town of Altamaha. Discrimination is unjust and illegal behavior toward people based on differences in race, religion, age, or gender (sex).

**A.** Read about the Civil Rights Act of 1964.

> Civil rights are the rights guaranteed to citizens to be treated equally under the law. The Civil Rights Act of 1964 was passed under President Lyndon Johnson. These laws were passed as a way to try to improve the lives of African Americans and other minority groups in this country.
>
> The Civil Rights Act of 1964 did the following:
>
> Made it against the law to discriminate in hotels, motels, restaurants, theaters, and other public places
>
> Took away money from government programs that discriminated
>
> Made it illegal to discriminate when employing workers or stopping their work

**B.** With a partner, research one of the following famous civil rights leaders. Take notes as you read. Prepare a short report about the person's life and work. If possible, bring in pictures to share with your classmates.

- W. E. B. Du Bois
- Dr. Martin Luther King Jr.
- Rosa Parks
- Thurgood Marshall

# Writing Practice

## Write a Descriptive Paragraph

A good descriptive paragraph about a person includes these ideas:

- An interesting introductory sentence to get the reader's attention
- Adjectives that help the reader picture or imagine what the person looks like
- Details or examples that describe what the person does and what his or her abilities are

Look at this word web. It includes words that describe how John Jones looks, how he acts, and what he wants to do at the beginning of the story.

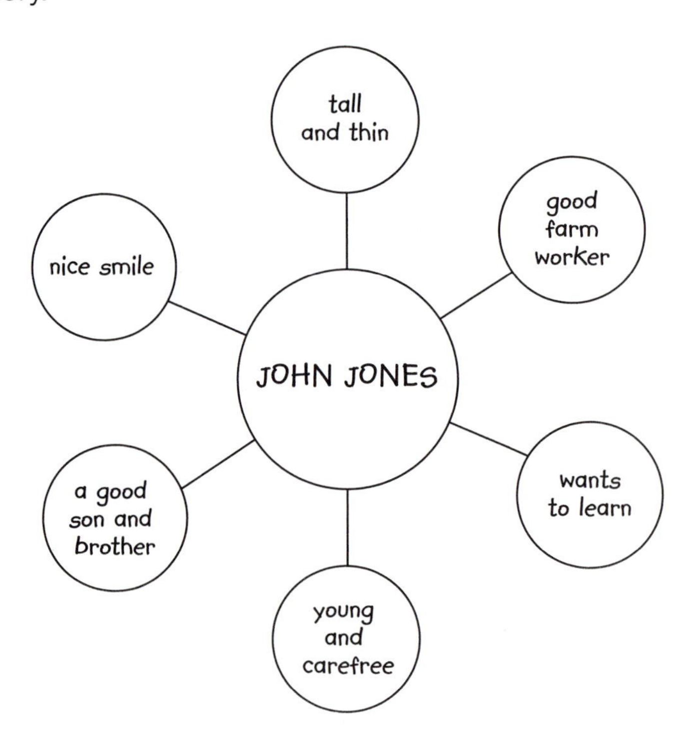


Write a paragraph describing someone you know. Think about the person you want to describe. What does he or she look like? What is special about the person? Make a word web to organize your ideas.

# 5

# The Lady, or the Tiger?

***Adapted from the story by Frank R. Stockton***

## *About the Author*

Frank R. Stockton was born in 1834. His most famous stories are in the form of fairy tales, ghost stories, or romances. But in all of them his humor has an edge like a knife. When "The Lady, or the Tiger?" appeared in *Century Magazine* in 1882, it caused excitement all over the country. Hundreds of people wrote letters to the magazine or to their newspapers about it. Many letters demanded an answer to the question that the story asks. Others asked if the story was really about government, psychology, the battle of the sexes, or something else. Wisely, Stockton never answered any of the letters. The story remains as fresh today as it was then. Frank Stockton died in 1902.

# Before You Read

## About "The Lady, or the Tiger?"

**Characters**
The young man, the princess, the semi-barbaric king

**Plot**
A princess has to decide whether to send her lover to the door with the lady behind it or the door with the tiger behind it. Either way, the princess loses him.

**Setting**
*Time:* a long, long time ago
*Place:* the king's arena

**Theme**
Love and jealousy are two powerful emotions. But which is more powerful?

## Build Background

### Imagine How the Story Ends

The story you are about to read ends with a question. Have you ever read a story or seen a movie that ends without telling you exactly what happens? At the end of "The Lady, or the Tiger?" you will have to imagine what happens. As you read this story, decide what you think will happen. Support your idea by what the author tells you about each character.

## Key Words

Read these sentences. Try to understand each word in dark type by looking at the other words in the sentence. Use a dictionary to check your ideas. Write each word and its meaning in your notebook.

accused
chance
imagination
jealous
semi-barbaric

1. A man was **accused** of a crime. But, in fact, the man had done nothing wrong.
2. Behind one door was a lady; behind the other door was a tiger. Only **chance,** or luck, could help the man choose the correct door.
3. An author can use her **imagination.** She can picture things in her mind that are not really there.
4. Sometimes the young woman was **jealous** and wanted what someone else had or wanted.
5. There once was a **semi-barbaric** king. He followed the rules of polite behavior only half the time.

## Reading Strategy

### Visualize

**Visualizing** means imagining, or picturing, something in your mind. Authors want readers to visualize the characters, events, and places in a story. Authors use descriptive words to help readers visualize. Often the descriptive words are adjectives. But verbs, nouns, and adverbs can also be descriptive.

- She was the *finest* and *most beautiful* lady. (adjectives)
- The happy bells *rang* and women *cried.* (verbs)
- He could turn the *dreams* of his *imagination* into *facts.* (nouns)
- He loved his daughter *deeply* and watched her *closely.* (adverbs)

As you read, try to visualize the characters, places, and events.

# The Lady, or the Tiger?

*Adapted from the story by Frank R. Stockton*

A long, long time ago, there was a semi-barbaric king. I call him semi-barbaric because the modern world, with its modern ideas, had softened his barbarism a little. But still, his ideas were large, wild, and free. He had a wonderful imagination. He was also a king of the greatest powers, and he easily turned the dreams of his imagination into facts. He greatly enjoyed talking to himself about ideas. And, when he and himself agreed upon a thing, the thing was done. He was a very pleasant man when everything in his world moved smoothly. And when something went wrong, he became even more pleasant. Nothing, you see, pleased him more than making wrong things right.

One of this semi-barbaric king's modern ideas was the idea of a large arena. In this arena, his people could watch both men and animals in acts of bravery.

But even this modern idea was touched by the king's wild imagination. In his arena, the people saw more than soldiers fighting soldiers, or men fighting animals. They enjoyed more than the sight of blood. In the king's arena, the people saw the laws of the country at work. They saw good men lifted up and bad men pushed down. Most important, they were able to watch the workings of the First Law of Chance.

Here is what happened when a man was accused of a crime. If the king was interested in the crime, then the people were told to come to the arena. They came together and sat there, thousands of them. The king sat high up in his king's chair. When he gave a sign, a door below him opened. The accused man stepped out into the arena. Across from him, on the other side of the arena, were two other doors. They were close together and they looked the same. The accused man would walk straight to these doors and open one of them. He could choose either one of the doors. He was forced by nothing and led by no one. Only Chance helped him—or didn't help him.

Behind one of the doors was a tiger. It was the wildest, biggest, hungriest tiger that could be found. Of course, it quickly jumped on the man. The man quickly—or not so quickly—died. After he died, sad bells rang, women cried, and the thousands of people walked home slowly.

But, if the accused man opened the other door, a lady would step out. She was the finest and most beautiful lady who could be found.

At that moment, there in the arena, she would be married to the man. It didn't matter if the man was already married. It didn't matter if he was in love with another woman. The king did not let little things like that get in the way of his imagination. No, the two were married there in front of the king. There was music and dancing. Then happy bells rang, women cried, and the thousands of people walked home singing.

This was the way the law worked in the king's semi-barbaric country. Its fairness is clear. The criminal could not know which door the lady was behind. He opened either door as he wanted. At the moment he opened the door, he did not know if he was going to be eaten or married.

The people of the country thought the law was a good one. They went to the arena with great interest. They never knew if they would see a bloody killing or a lovely marriage. This uncertainty gave the day its fine and unusual taste. And they liked the fairness of the law. Wasn't it true that the accused man held his life in his own hands?

This semi-barbaric king had a daughter. The princess was as beautiful as any flower in the king's imagination. She had a mind as wild and free as the king's. She had a heart like a volcano. The king loved her deeply, watched her closely, and was very jealous of her. But he could not always watch her. And in his castle lived a young man. This young man was a worker. He was a good worker, but he was of low birth. He was brave and handsome, and the princess loved him, and was jealous of him. Because of the girl's semi-barbarism, her love was hot and strong. Of course, the young man quickly returned it. The lovers were happy together for many months. But one day the king discovered their love. Of course he did not lose a minute. He threw the young man into prison and named a day for his appearance in the arena.

There had never been a day as important as that one. The country was searched for the strongest, biggest, most dangerous tiger. With equal care, the country was searched for the finest and most beautiful young woman. There was no question, of course, that the young man had loved the princess. He knew it, she knew it, the king knew it, and everybody else knew it, too. But the king didn't let this stand in the way of his excellent law. Also, the king knew that the young man would now disappear from his daughter's life. He would disappear with the other beautiful lady. Or he would disappear into the hungry tiger. The only question was, "Which?"

And so the day arrived. Thousands and thousands of people came to the arena. The king was in his place, across from those two doors that seemed alike but were truly very different.

All was ready. The sign was given. The door below the king opened, and the lover of the princess walked into the arena. Tall, handsome, fair, he seemed like a prince. The people had not known that such a fine young man had lived among them. Was it any wonder that the princess had loved him?

The young man came forward into the arena, and then turned toward the king's chair. But his eyes were not on the king. They were on the princess, who sat to her father's right. Perhaps it was wrong for the young lady to be there. But remember that she was still semi-barbaric. Her wild heart would not let her be away from her lover on this day. More important, she now knew the secret of the doors. Over the past few days, she had used all of her power in the castle, and much of her gold. She had discovered which door hid the tiger, and which door hid the lady.

She knew more than this. She knew the lady. It was one of the fairest and loveliest ladies in the castle. In fact, this lady was more than fair and lovely. She was thoughtful, kind, loving, full of laughter, and quick of mind. The princess hated her. She had seen, or imagined she had seen, the lady looking at the young man. She thought these looks had been noticed and even returned. Once or twice she had seen them talking together. Perhaps they had talked for only a moment. Perhaps they had talked of nothing important. But how could the princess be sure of that? The other girl was lovely and kind, yes. But she had lifted her eyes to the lover of the princess.

And so, in her semi-barbaric heart, the princess was jealous, and hated her.

Now, in the arena, her lover turned and looked at her. His eyes met hers, and he saw at once that she knew the secret of the doors. He had been sure that she would know it. He understood her heart. He had known that she would try to learn this thing which no one else knew—not even the king. He had known she would try. And now, as he looked at her, he saw that she had succeeded.

At that moment, his quick and worried look asked the question: "Which?" This question in his eyes was as clear to the princess as spoken words. There was no time to lose. The question had been asked in a second. It must be answered in a second.

Her right arm rested on the arm of her chair. She lifted her hand and made a quick movement toward the right. No one saw except her lover. Every eye except his was on the man in the arena.

He turned and walked quickly across the empty space. Every heart stopped beating. Every breath was held. Every eye was fixed upon that man. Without stopping for even a second, he went to the door on the right and opened it.

Now, the question is this: Did the tiger come out of that door, or did the lady?

As we think deeply about this question, it becomes harder and harder to answer. We must know the heart of the animal called man. And the heart is difficult to know. Think of it, dear reader, and remember that the decision is not yours. The decision belongs to that hot-blooded, semi-barbaric princess. Her heart was at a white heat beneath the fires of jealousy and painful sadness. She had lost him, but who should have him?

Very often, in her thoughts and in her dreams, she had cried out in fear. She had imagined her lover as he opened the door to the hungry tiger.

And even more often she had seen him at the other door! She had bitten her tongue and pulled her hair. She had hated his happiness when he opened the door to the lady. Her heart burned

with pain and hatred when she imagined the scene: He goes quickly to meet the woman. He leads her into the arena. His eyes shine with new life. The happy bells ring wildly. The two of them are married before her eyes. Children run around them and throw flowers. There is music, and the thousands of people dance in the streets. And the princess's cry of sadness is lost in the sounds of happiness!

Wouldn't it be better for him to die at once? Couldn't he wait for her in the beautiful land of the semi-barbaric future?

But the tiger, those cries of pain, that blood!

Her decision had been shown in a second. But it had been made after days and nights of deep and painful thought. She had known she would be asked. She had decided what to answer. She had moved her hand to the right.

The question of her decision is not an easy one to think about. Certainly I am not the one person who should have to answer it. So I leave it with all of you: Which came out of the opened door—the lady, or the tiger?

# After You Read

## Understand the Story

Answer these questions in your notebook. Write complete sentences.

1. When did this story take place?
2. What happened after an accused man was killed by a tiger?
3. Why did the people of the country think "the lady or the tiger" law was a good one?
4. How did the princess discover the secret of the doors?
5. Why did the princess hate the young lady behind the door?
6. Why did no one except the young man see the princess move her hand to the right?

## Elements of Literature

### Sensory Details

**Sensory details** are words or phrases that describe how things look, feel, sound, smell, and taste (our five senses). They help us picture what the author is telling us about. Read these sentences from the story. Then answer the questions.

> Behind one of the doors was a tiger. It was the wildest, biggest, hungriest tiger that could be found. Of course, it quickly jumped on the man. The man quickly—or not so quickly—died. After he died, sad bells rang, women cried, and the thousands of people walked home slowly.

What words does the author use to describe what happened when someone chose the door with the tiger behind it? Which words help you see and hear the event in your mind?

## Discussion

Discuss in pairs or small groups.

1. Do you think the princess sent the young man to the lady or to the tiger? Why?

2. If you were the young man, would you have opened the door on the right? Why or why not?

3. Have you ever had to decide between two choices? How did you decide? Did you make the right decision?

## Vocabulary

Choose the correct word. Write the completed sentences in your notebook.

1. The king was only ______ because the modern world had softened him a little.
   **a.** handsome **b.** imagination **c.** semi-barbaric

2. Every idea was touched by the king's wild and wonderful ______.
   **a.** arena **b.** imagination **c.** jealousy

3. The princess was ______ of the other girl, and hated her.
   **a.** jealous **b.** accused **c.** semi-barbaric

4. Another word for luck is ______.
   **a.** fair **b.** good **c.** chance

5. The ______ man stepped out into the arena.
   **a.** jealous **b.** accused **c.** semi-barbaric

## Word Study

Sometimes the noun form of a word is very different from the verb and adjective forms. Look at the examples in the chart.

Write the sentences below in your notebook. Complete each sentence with the correct form of the word. Use the chart to help you. The first item has been done for you.

| Noun | Verb | Adjective |
|---|---|---|
| marriage | marry | married |
| accusation | accuse | accused |
| imagination | imagine | imaginative |
| success | succeed | successful |

1. Although the princess loved the young man, the king was against their __marriage__. **marriage/married**

2. If a man chose the door with the lady behind it, he had to ________ the lady. **marriage/marry**

3. The ________ man had to open one of the doors. **accusation/accused**

4. The king was an ________ man. **imagine/imaginative**

5. The king's laws were like his wild ________. **imagination/imaginative**

6. Can you ________ how the princess felt? **imagination/imagine**

7. The princess does ________ in giving the young man a sign. But we don't know whether she saved his life or not. **success/succeed**

## Extension Activity

### Chance

In life, some events have a better or worse chance of happening. Some events have an equal chance of happening. In the story "The Lady, or the Tiger?" the young man had to choose between two doors. He had an equal chance of choosing the lady or the tiger.

**A.** When people predict, they guess about the chance that something will happen. Here are some words people use when they predict:

- If something is **certain** to happen, it will happen.
- If something is **impossible,** it cannot happen.
- If something is **likely,** it probably will happen.
- If something is **unlikely,** it probably won't happen.

**B.** Read the sentences and copy them into your notebook. Predict whether each event will happen. Write *certain, impossible, likely,* or *unlikely* next to each sentence.

1. Tomorrow, your ears will become wings.
2. On a clear night, you can see stars in the sky.
3. At noon, it will be dark.
4. My favorite team will win a ball game.
5. There will be waves in the ocean.
6. A tiger will visit my school.
7. The seed I planted will grow.
8. A wish I made will come true.

## Writing Practice

### Write an Opinion

When you write an opinion, you tell your thoughts or feelings about a subject.

- An opinion is not a fact.
- An opinion cannot be proved.
- An opinion can be supported (made stronger) by facts or details.

Read the question below. Then read the paragraph that states an opinion and gives three reasons that support the opinion.

> *Question:* "Which came out of the opened door—the lady, or the tiger?"
>
> *Opinion:* I think it was the lady who came out. If the princess really loved the young man, she would have wanted him to live. Even though she would not be able to marry him, she still might be able to see him. Then she would feel happy knowing that he was alive and well, and that she had saved his life.

Now, complete the opinion that begins below. Write the opinion in your notebook and give reasons to support the opinion.

> *Opinion:* I think it was the tiger that came out.

6

# How I Went to the Mines

***Adapted from the story by Bret Harte***

## *About the Author*

Bret Harte was born in Albany, New York, in 1836. His father was a teacher who died young. His mother remarried and moved to San Francisco. When Harte was seventeen, he joined his mother and her second husband. In California, Harte turned to writing after trying several other jobs. For a while he was an unsuccessful gold miner. His story "How I Went to the Mines" came from that experience. In 1868, he published a story, "The Luck of Roaring Camp." The story brought him national fame. Suddenly famous, he went East to write for the *Atlantic Monthly* magazine for $10,000 a year (a very large amount in those days). But his success and his popularity as a writer did not last long. As a result, Harte left the United States in 1877 to work as a businessman and U.S. consul in Europe. He finally settled in England in 1885, where he lived and continued to publish books until his death in 1902.

# Before You Read

## About "How I Went to the Mines"

**Characters**
A young schoolmaster, a stranger, three miners

**Plot**
A young man loses his position as a schoolmaster and goes to the mines to try to find gold. Three partners take him in and teach him to mine.

**Setting**
*Time:* after 1848, during the California gold rush
*Place:* California

**Theme**
A young person can follow the American dream of working hard and being successful.

## Build Background

### The California Gold Rush

In January of 1848, a man named James Marshall found some gold nuggets near a river in Sacramento, California. Soon after, two other men discovered gold. Those discoveries were the beginning of what is called "the California gold rush." About half a million people from different states and other countries "rushed" to California to search for gold. With so many new people, California became another state in the United States in 1850. By 1864, the gold rush was over.

If you had lived in 1848, would you have wanted to go to the mines to look for gold? Why or why not?

## Key Words

Read these sentences. Try to understand the words in dark type by looking at the other words in the sentence. Use a dictionary to check your ideas. Write each word and its meaning in your notebook.

claim
mines
nuggets
pan
partners
pick
pioneers
quartz
shovel

1. Miners marked the area they mined, their **claim,** with a sign and listed the claim at a government office.
2. Many men worked in **mines,** places from which gold, metals, and other precious stones are taken.
3. Miners were excited when they saw shiny **nuggets**—small gold pieces.
4. Miners placed dirt in a **pan,** a large, shallow container.
5. Miners often worked with **partners,** other men who could help them mine a large area.
6. Miners used a **pick,** a tool with a sharp metal point, to break the ground.
7. **Pioneers** were the people who first settled the West.
8. The miners found many white stones called **quartz.**
9. Miners used a **shovel** to lift the dirt.

## Reading Strategy

### Skim

**Skimming** a text means reading it very quickly to get a general idea of what it is about. To skim a story, follow these steps:

- Read the first and second paragraphs quickly.
- Read only the first sentences of the following paragraphs.
- Read the last paragraph quickly.

# How I Went to the Mines

*Adapted from the story by Bret Harte*

## I

I had been in California for two years before I thought of going to the mines. My introduction to gold digging was partly forced on me. I was the somewhat youthful and, I fear, not very experienced schoolmaster of a small pioneer settlement. Our school was only partly paid for by the state; most of the cost was carried by a few families in the settlement. When two families—and about a dozen children—moved away to a richer and newer district, the school was immediately closed.

In twenty-four hours, I was without both students and employment. I am afraid I missed the children the most: I had made companions and friends of some of them. I stood that bright May morning before an empty schoolhouse in the wild woods. I felt strange to think that our little summer "play" at being schoolmaster and student was over. I remember clearly a parting gift from a student a year older than I. He gave me a huge piece of gingerbread. It helped me greatly in my journeys, for I was alone in the world at that moment, and by nature extravagant with money.

I had been frightfully extravagant even on my small schoolmaster's pay. I had spent much money on fine shirts. I gave as an excuse that I should set an example in dress for my students. The result, however, was that at this important moment, I had only seven dollars in my pocket. I spent five on a secondhand revolver that I felt was necessary to show that I was leaving peaceful employment for one of risk and adventure.

For I had finally decided to go to the mines and become a gold digger. Other employment, and my few friends in San Francisco, were expensively distant. The nearest mining district was only forty miles away. My hope was that when I got there I would find a miner named Jim I had met once in San Francisco. With only his name to help me, I expected to find him somewhere in the mines. But my remaining two dollars was not enough for travel by horse and wagon. I must walk to the mines, and I did.

I cannot clearly remember *how* I did it. The end of the first day found me with painfully blistered feet. I realized that the shiny leather shoes, so proper for a schoolmaster, were not suited to my wanderings. But I held on to them as a sign of my past life. I carried them in my hands when pain and pride caused me to leave the highway and travel barefoot on the trails.

I'm afraid all my belongings looked unsuitable. The few travelers I met on the road looked at me and tried not to smile. I had a fine old leather bag my mother had given me, and a silver-handled whip—also a gift. These did not exactly suit the rough blue blanket and tin coffee pot I carried with them. To my embarrassment, my revolver would not stay properly in its holster at my side. It kept working its way around to where it hung down in front.

I was too proud to arrive at Jim's door penniless, so I didn't stop at any hotels along the way. I ate my gingerbread and camped out in the woods. The loneliness I felt once or twice along the road completely disappeared in the sweet and silent companionship of the woods. I wasn't aware of hunger, and I slept soundly, quite forgetting the pain of my blistered feet. In the morning I found I had emptied my water bottle. I also found I had completely overlooked the first rule of camping—to settle near water. But I chewed some unboiled coffee beans for breakfast, and again took up the trail.

The pine-filled air, the distant view of mountains, led me onward. I was excited to see strange, white pieces of rock, shining like teeth against the red dirt. This was called *quartz,* I had been told. Quartz was a sign of a gold mining district. At about sunset I came out of the pines and looked across at a mountain side covered with white tents. They stuck up out of the earth like the white quartz. It was the "diggings"!

I do not know what I had expected, but I was disappointed. As I looked across at the mining camp, the sun set. A great shadow covered the tents, and a number of tiny lights, like stars, shone in their place. A cold wind rushed down the mountainside. I felt cold in my clothes, wet from a long day's journey. It was nine o'clock when I reached the mining camp. I had been on my feet since sunrise. But I hid my belongings in the bushes, and washed my feet in a stream of water. I put on my terrible leather shoes and limped, in my painful pride, to the first miner's log cabin. Here I learned that Jim was one of four partners who worked a claim two miles away, on the other side of the mountain. There was nothing for me to do but go on. I would find the Magnolia Hotel. I would buy the cheapest food, rest an hour, and then limp painfully, as best I could, to Jim's claim.

## II

The Magnolia Hotel was a large wooden building. The greater part was given over to a huge drinking saloon. Shining mirrors hung on the walls, and a long bar ran down one side of the room. In the unimportant dining room I ordered fish-balls and coffee because they were cheap and quick. The waiter told me that my friend Jim might live in the settlement. The barkeeper, though, knew everything and everybody, and would tell me the shortest way to his log cabin.

I was very tired. I'm afraid I took a longer time over my food than was proper. Then I went into the saloon. It was crowded with miners and traders and a few well-dressed businessmen. Here again my pride led me to extravagance. I was ashamed to ask the important, white-shirted and diamond-pinned barkeeper for information, without buying a drink. I'm afraid I laid down another quarter on the bar. I asked my question, and the barkeeper passed me a bottle and glass. Suddenly a strange thing happened. As it had some effect on my future, I will tell you about it here.

The ceiling of the saloon was held up by a half-dozen tall wooden posts. They stood in front of the bar, about two feet from it.

The front of the bar was crowded with drinkers. Suddenly, to my surprise, they all put down their glasses and hurriedly backed into the spaces behind the posts. At the same moment a shot was fired through the large open doors that opened into the saloon.

The bullet hit the bar and broke off pieces of wood. The shot was returned from the upper end of the bar. And then for the first time I realized that two men with revolvers were shooting at each other across the saloon.

The other men were hiding behind the posts; the barkeeper was down behind the bar. Six shots were fired by the revolvers. As far as I could see nobody was hurt. A mirror was broken, and my glass had been hit by the third shot. But the whole thing passed so quickly, and I was so surprised by it all, that I cannot remember feeling afraid. My only worry was that I would show to the others my youth, inexperience, or shock. I think any shy, proud young man will understand this, and would probably feel as I did. So strong was this feeling that while the smell of the gunpowder was still in my nose, I spoke out. I picked up the broken glass, and said to the barkeeper slowly, coolly, "Will you please fill me another glass? It's not my fault if this one was broken."

The barkeeper stood up behind the bar. His face was red and excited. He gave me a strange smile and passed me the bottle and a fresh glass. I heard a laugh behind me, and was embarrassed. I took a large gulp of the drink and hurried to leave. But my blistered feet hurt, and I could only limp to the door. I felt a hand on my back. A voice said quickly, "You're not hurt, old man?" I recognized the man who had laughed. My face felt hot and red. I answered quickly that my feet were blistered from a long walk. I was in a hurry to get to Jim's claim.

"Hold on," said the stranger. He went out to the street and called to a man in a horse and wagon. "Drop him," he said, pointing at me, "at Jim's cabin, and then come back here." Then he helped me into the wagon. He slapped me on the back, and said mysteriously, "You'll do!" Then he returned quickly to the saloon.

I learned from the driver about the gun fight. Two men had had a wild argument the week before. They had sworn to shoot each other "on sight"—that is, at their next meeting. They were going around with revolvers ready. The driver added that the men seemed to be "pretty bad shooters." And I, knowing nothing of these deadly weapons, and thinking pretty much what he thought, agreed! I said nothing of my own feelings, though, and soon forgot them. For as we came near to Jim's log cabin, I had reached the end of my journey.

## III

Now, for the first time I began to have doubts about my plan: to ask help and advice from a man I hardly knew. I believe it is a common experience of youth that during the journey I had never felt doubts. But *now,* as I arrived, my youth and inexperience came to me like a shock. And it was followed by a greater one. When at last I left my driver and entered the small log cabin, Jim's partners told me that he had left the partnership and gone back to San Francisco.

Perhaps I looked tired and disappointed. One of the partners pulled out the only chair and offered me a drink. With encouragement, I limped through my story. I think I told the exact truth. I was even too tired to make it sound as if Jim and I were really friends.

They listened without speaking. Probably they had heard such stories before. I expect they had gone through a harder experience than mine. Then something happened that I am sure could have happened only in California in that time of simplicity and confidence. Without a word of discussion among themselves, without a word to ask about my character or experience, they offered me Jim's partnership, "to try."

I went to bed that night in Jim's bunk bed. I was one-fourth owner of a log cabin and a claim I knew nothing about. I looked around me at the three bearded faces, only a few years older than I.

I wondered if we were playing at being miners as I had played at being a schoolmaster.

I awoke late the next morning and stared around the empty cabin. I could hardly believe that what had happened the night before wasn't a dream. The cabin was made of pine logs with four bunk beds on two sides. Bright sunlight streamed in through *holes* in the walls. There was a table and chair, and three old boxes for furniture. There was one window beside the open door, and a fireplace at the other end. I was wondering if I had moved into an empty cabin, when my partners entered. They had let me sleep—It was twelve o'clock! My breakfast was ready. They had something funny to tell me—I was a hero!

My behavior during the shooting match at the Magnolia saloon was being discussed and reported by men who had been there. The story was wildly enlarged. They said I had stood coolly at the bar, quietly demanding a drink while the shots were being fired! I told my partners the truth, but I am afraid they didn't believe me. They thought I was young enough to be embarrassed by being noticed, and they changed the subject.

Yes, they said, I could go digging that day. Where? Oh, anywhere on ground that was not already claimed. There were hundreds of square miles to choose from. How to do it? You mean, you have never mined before? Never dug for gold at all? Never! I saw them look quickly at each other. My heart sank. But I noticed that their eyes were bright and happy. Then I learned that my inexperience was considered lucky. Gold miners believed in "beginner's luck," the unexplained luck that came to first-time miners. But I must choose a place to dig myself, to make the luck work.

I was given a pick and shovel, and a pan to wash the gold nuggets from the dirt. I decided to dig on a grassy hillside about two hundred yards from the cabin. They told me to fill my pan with dirt around a large area. In one or two shovels-full I dug up some pieces of shining quartz, and put them hopefully in my pocket. Then I filled my pan. I carried it with difficulty—it was surprisingly

heavy—to the stream to wash it. As I moved the pan back and forth in the running water, the red dirt washed away. Only stones and black sand were left. I picked out the stones with my fingers, and kept only a small flat, pretty, round stone. It looked like a coin. I put it in my pocket with the quartz. Then I washed away the black sand. You can imagine how I felt when I saw a dozen tiny gold stars in the bottom of the pan! They were so small that I was afraid I would wash them away. I learned later that they are so heavy that there is very little danger of that. I ran happily to where my partners were working.

"Yes, he's got the 'color,'" one said without excitement. "I knew it."

I was disappointed. "Then I haven't struck gold?" I said shyly.

"Not in *this* pan. You've only got a quarter of a dollar there. But," he continued with a smile, "you only have to get that much in four pans, and you've made enough for your daily food."

"And that's all any of us—or anyone on this claim—have made in the last six months!" another partner said.

This was another shock to me. But he spoke with good humor and youthful carelessness. I took comfort from that. But I was still disappointed by my first try. I shyly pulled the quartz out of my pocket.

"I found these," I said. "They look as if they have gold in them. See how it shines?"

My partner smiled. "That's worthless. Those are iron pyrites, called 'fool's gold.' But what's that?" he added quickly. He took the round flat stone from my hand, "Where did you find that?"

"In the same hole as the quartz. Is it good for anything?"

He did not answer, but turning to the other partners who were coming over to see, he said, "Look!"

He laid my stone on another stone and hit it with his pick. I was surprised that it didn't break. Where the pick had hit it, it showed a bright yellow star!

I had no time, or need, to ask another question. "Write out a claim notice!" he said to one partner. And, "Run, get a post!" to the other. We put the notice on the post, to announce our claim, and began to dig madly.

The gold nugget I had picked up was worth about twelve dollars. We carried many pans, we worked that day and the next hopefully, happily, and without tiring. Then we worked at the claim daily, carefully, and regularly for three weeks. Sometimes we found the "color," and sometimes we didn't. But we nearly always got enough for our daily food. We laughed, joked, told stories and enjoyed ourselves as if we were at an endless picnic. But that twelve-dollar nugget was the first and last find we made on the new, "Beginner's Luck" claim!

# After You Read

## Understand the Story

Answer these questions in your notebook. Write complete sentences.

1. At the beginning of the story, what was the narrator doing in California?
2. What did he decide to do next? Why?
3. How did he travel? Why?
4. When the gunfight broke out in the saloon, why didn't the narrator hide? Why did he ask for a new glass?
5. Why were the young man's new partners happy that he had no mining experience?

## Elements of Literature

### Point of View

Who tells a story determines the story's **point of view.** The narrator of "How I Went to the Mines" is also the main character. He tells his own story. He refers to himself using the word *I*. This point of view is called first person. The following passage is the beginning of the narrator's description of his walk to the mines:

> I cannot clearly remember *how* I did it. The end of the first day left me with painfully blistered feet. I realized that the shiny leather shoes, so proper for a schoolmaster, were not suited to my wanderings. But I held on to them as a sign of my past life. I carried them in my hands when pain and pride caused me to leave the highway and travel barefoot on the trails.

Notice how the narrator tells the reader details about his feelings and thoughts as he moves along the story's plot. We can see the same point of view in Poe's "The Tell-Tale Heart" and Twain's "A Cub-Pilot's Education."

## Discussion

Discuss in pairs or small groups.

What do you think of the narrator in "How I Went to the Mines"? In what ways is he strong? In what ways is he brave? In what ways is he silly?

## Vocabulary

Choose the correct word. Write the completed sentences in your notebook.

**1.** I was the schoolmaster of a small settlement of ______.
**a.** shovels **b.** claims **c.** pioneers

**2.** I decided to go to the ______ and become a gold digger.
**a.** quartz **b.** mines **c.** nuggets

**3.** Jim was one of four ______ who worked together.
**a.** claims **b.** partners **c.** picks

**4.** I saw white pieces of rock called ______.
**a.** quartz **b.** mines **c.** pioneers

**5.** I saw a dozen tiny gold stars in the bottom of the ______.
**a.** pan **b.** partner **c.** pick

**6.** I used my new ______ to dig for gold.
**a.** mine **b.** nugget **c.** shovel

**7.** He laid my stone on another stone and hit it with his ______.
**a.** pan **b.** pick **c.** pioneer

**8.** We put the notice on the post to announce our ______.
**a.** claim **b.** pan **c.** shovel

**9.** I picked up a gold ______ worth twelve dollars.
**a.** quartz **b.** partner **c.** nugget

## Word Study

Write the sentences below in your notebook. Complete each sentence with the correct form of the word. Use the chart to help you. The first item has been done for you.

| Noun | Adjective |
|---|---|
| employment | employed |
| embarrassment | embarrassed |
| disappointment | disappointed |
| encouragement | encouraged |
| confidence | confident |

1. The small pioneer school closed. So the young man was without ___employment___.
   **employment/employed**

2. The young man was ____________ that his revolver
   **embarrassment/embarrassed**
   would not stay at his side.

3. The young man's red face showed his ____________
   **embarrassment/embarrassed**
   when the man laughed at him.

4. He was ____________ when he first saw the
   **disappointment/disappointed**
   mining camp.

5. With ____________, the young man told Jim's
   **encouragement/encouraged**
   partners his whole story.

6. Jim's partners were ____________ that the young man
   **confidence/confident**
   would be a good addition to their partnership.

# Extension Activity

## The California Gold Rush

As you have read, gold was discovered in California in 1848. The gold rush continued for the next 16 years. Some miners found gold and became rich. And, the new state of California grew and grew.

**A.** Read about a clever businessman.

Once gold was discovered in California, a man named Sam Brannan became one of the richest men in California. He never mined for gold. Sam Brannan made his money by selling picks, pans, and shovels. And, Sam Brannan was a clever businessman. Just as the gold rush began, he raised the prices on all the mining equipment he sold, and he made lots of money.

**B.** Imagine you lived in California during the gold rush and owned a shop. Now hundreds of people are coming through your town. This is your chance to be a smart shopkeeper. Work with a partner. Think about all the things you might want to sell to the new Californians. Write and illustrate an advertisement that shows all the things that are for sale in your shop.

# Writing Practice

## Write a Personal Narrative

In a personal narrative, a writer tells a story from his or her own experience.

- A personal narrative can be fiction.
- The events of the narrative are usually told in time order.
- The writer gives details of each event to give the reader a clear picture of what happened.

Look at this timeline about "How I Went to the Mines."

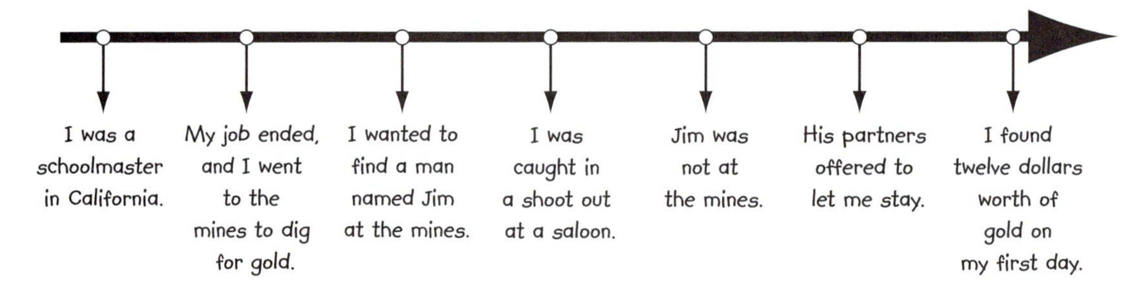


Write a personal narrative about a time when you were successful at something you tried to do. Make a timeline of the important events you want to tell about. When you write, include many details about each event so that the reader can get a clear picture.

# Glossary

**adjective:** word that describes someone or something: *The tree has green leaves. She is a good writer.*

**adverb:** word that tells you how, when, or where something is done: *The boy ran quickly.*

**author:** person who writes a story; writer

**author's purpose:** author's reason for writing something, such as to entertain the reader or to teach the reader

**cause and effect:** A cause is why something happens. An effect is what happens. A cause makes an effect happen.

**comparison:** words that tell how two things are alike

**characterization:** how an author creates a character

**characters:** people or animals in a story

**critic:** person who gives his or her opinion of something; reviewer

**description:** words that describe someone or something, or tell what someone or something is like

**foreshadowing:** an author's hints about what will happen in a story

**horror story:** story written to frighten, or scare, the reader. "The Tell-Tale Heart" is a horror story.

**infer:** make guesses about the meaning of something based on clues or facts; make inferences

**interview:** a talk in which one person asks questions and writes down the other person's answers

**irony:** when what happens is the opposite of what you expect

**journal entry:** piece of writing in which you tell your thoughts and feelings about events in your life

**make inferences:** make guesses about the meaning of something based on clues or facts, infer

**mood:** feeling that a piece of writing gives you. A mood can be sad, scary, or funny, for example.

**narrator:** person telling the story. The narrator is sometimes a character in the story.

**noun:** word that names something or someone. *My father is a teacher. The bird sings.*

**opinion:** a person's thoughts and feelings about a subject

**personal narrative:** piece of writing in which you tell a story from your own experience

**plot:** what happens in a story; the action of a story

**point of view:** the way a story is presented. First-person point of view is when a narrator tells a story using *I* and *my.*

**predict:** guess what will happen

**review:** a piece of writing in which you say whether you liked something, such as a book or a movie, and give reasons why

**reviewer:** person who gives his or her opinion of something, critic

**sensory details:** words that describe how things look, feel, sound, smell, or taste (our five senses)

**setting:** when and where the story happens; time and place of the story's action

**short story:** short work of fiction that has characters, plot, setting, and sometimes a theme

**skimming:** reading quickly to get a general idea of what a text is about

**surprise ending:** story ending in which the plot takes a sudden turn

**suspense:** feeling of excitement and curiosity about what will happen next in a story

**theme:** a general idea about life that the author communicates through the story

**verb:** word that describes an action *(The birds flew south)* or a state *(I am hungry)*

**visualize:** picture something in your mind

# Index